I0168096

FINDING COURAGE

A Four-Week Devotional Journey

Steve A. Brown

Author of best sellers
Jesus Centered and *Leading Me*

FINDING COURAGE
Copyright ©2025 Steve A. Brown

978-1-998815-40-1 Soft Cover
978-1-998815-41-8 E-book

Published by:
Castle Quay Books
Little Britain, Ontario, Canada
Jupiter, Florida, USA
Tel: (416) 573-3249
E-mail: info@castlequaybooks.com | www.castlequaybooks.com

Edited by Marina Hofman Willard PhD
Cover design and book interior by Burst Impressions

All rights reserved. This book or parts thereof may not be reproduced in any form without prior written permission of the publishers.

Scripture quotations taken from the Holy Bible, New International Version®, NIV® Copyright ©1973, 1978, 1984, 2011 by Biblica, Inc.® Used by permission. All rights reserved worldwide.

Excerpts from or references to Steve A. Brown's earlier books, *Jesus Centered* and *Leading Me* are used with permission.

Thank you to Arrow Leadership for permission to excerpt some concepts and content from my years writing the e-resources at www.sharpeningleaders.com.

Library and Archives Canada Cataloguing in Publication
Title: Finding courage : a four-week devotional journey / written by Steve A. Brown.
Names: Brown, Steve A., 1970- author.
Identifiers: Canadiana 20250183153 | ISBN 9781998815401 (softcover)
Subjects: LCSH: Courage—Prayers and devotions. | LCSH: Devotional calendars. | LCGFT: Devotional
    literature.
Classification: LCC BV4811 .B76 2025 | DDC 242/.2—dc23

CASTLE QUAY BOOKS

To students of Columbia Bible College
and this next generation:
keep leaning into your faith and seeking to
launch your lives in ways that glorify God.

It's inspiring to watch you and a joy to cheer you on!

WEEK
ONE

1.

START HERE

> Be strong and courageous. Do not be afraid;
> do not be discouraged, for the Lᴏʀᴅ your God
> will be with you wherever you go. (Joshua 1:9)

DO YOU NEED more courage? How might you live today differently if you lived with more courage?

Most people need more courage in some area of their lives. Sometimes courage is needed in everyday moments or in events you might not even see coming. Sometimes courage is needed in long, grinding seasons when there seems to be no end in sight.

Faithfully following Jesus also requires courage. Speaking the truth in love in a post-truth culture requires courage. Stepping out in faithful obedience to Jesus requires courage. Standing up for the marginalized and against injustice requires courage. Faithfully pointing others to Jesus requires courage.

You might need courage to speak boldly or to be quiet and listen. You might need courage to step forward, patiently wait, or graciously step back. You might need the courage to say yes, no, or not now. You might need courage to dream, try a new idea, or stop something. You might need courage to take risks, obey, or keep pressing on in the midst of difficult circumstances. You might need courage to take a stand for truth or to invite help. You might need courage to reach out, to confront, or to forgive.

Courage is a big deal. Without courage, we end up letting fear, comfort, and even darkness win. It's hard to overstate the importance of courage. Living with courage means faithfully persevering and pressing on. With courage, there's possibility and potential. Without courage, there's fear, hesitation, status quo, limits, and even disobedience. As C. S. Lewis wrote in *The Screwtape Letters*, "Courage isn't simply one of the virtues, but the form of every virtue at the testing point."

But what is courage?

Here's one definition I've been working on for Jesus's followers: **Courage is choosing to follow Jesus even when your knees are knocking.**

Scripture, just like our lives, is filled with moments when fear battles with courage. I suspect Queen Esther's knees were knocking when she entered the king's court to advocate for her people. I imagine Nathan had clammy hands and a dry mouth when he confronted King David about his sin. I suspect Peter must have had a great internal battle in the courtyard when he denied being a disciple. I bet Ananias had serious second thoughts before he knocked at the door on Straight Street and asked for a man from Tarsus named Saul, who was known for persecuting Jews. In all these examples, the choice of obedience required courage.

"Do not fear" is one of the most popular phrases in Scripture for good reason. Like the ten fear-filled spies reporting back to Joshua about the Promised Land, we can feel like grasshoppers compared to what seem like giant challenges around us and within us. Instead, we need to take to heart the Lord's command to Joshua, "Be strong and courageous. Do not be afraid; do not be discouraged, for the LORD your God will be with you wherever you go" (Joshua 1:9).

This devotional is designed to help you find more courage, whether you are navigating the regular everyday, a crucible moment, a deep valley, a desert season, or a mountaintop. It's written in a daily devotional format because courage is a daily need, choice, and discipline. Over four weeks of daily reflections, you will receive a steady feed of biblically grounded encouragement and practical application.

Beyond finding more courage, we need to give more courage. Everyone you meet needs more courage in some area of their life, and Jesus's followers are called to be courage givers to others. To this end, the focus of each week's last entry shifts from finding more courage to being a courage giver to others.

In terms of format, each day starts with a Scripture followed by a short reflection. The Action and Reflection and Prayer segments give you the opportunity to apply and respond.

BOTTOM LINE

Courage is required to live life well and to follow Jesus faithfully. Courage is choosing not to let fear win. Courage is about choosing to follow Jesus even when your knees are knocking. Courage is something you can seek to give to others.

ACTION AND REFLECTION

Where do you need more courage right now? At home, work, or school? With finances, health, a relationship, or temptation? With uncertainty?

Who has been a courage giver in your life? How did they share courage?

PRAYER

(Inspired by Joshua 1:9 and Psalm 18)

Lord, as I start this devotional journey, I desire to be strong and courageous. I don't want to let fear win. I choose obedience and to faithfully follow You, even when my knees are knocking.

As I embark on this devotional journey, I pray that You will remind me day by day that You are with me.

Grow my courage as I come to a bigger, clearer, and fuller picture of and wholehearted trust in who You are.

Help me see others who need courage and be a courage giver.

I pray these things in the name of the One who is my strength, my rock, my fortress, my deliverer, my refuge, and my stronghold.

2.

CONSIDER HIM

Consider him who endured such opposition
from sinners, so that you will not grow weary
and lose heart. (Hebrews 12:3)

FEELING LIKE YOUR personal fuel gauge is near empty? Is your resolve starting to crumble in the face of fear or opposition?

In Matthew 16:24, Jesus told his disciples, "Whoever wants to be my disciple must deny themselves and take up their cross and follow me." Dietrich Bonhoeffer reminds us that on this path of learning to deny ourselves, "the cross means rejection and shame as well as suffering." Choosing and following this path is incredibly countercultural because it requires the rejection of our modern-day idols of personal safety and comfort. It's a path that may require great courage and may severely tax your physical, emotional, mental, and spiritual reserves.

Though this path is not easy, there is good news that can give you strength. For starters, there is someone who understands. His name is Jesus. He not only understands the space you are in, but He has also gone before you and modeled the way for you to follow. You can look to Jesus's example to give you courage today.

In my book, *Jesus Centered*, I shared this description of Jesus's example:

Day after day, Jesus faced incredible and sustained resistance. There were endless, needy crowds. There were cleverly laid traps to avoid and subtle temptations to resist. His disciples were slow learners and frequent on-the-job sleepers. He endured loneliness and profound internal distress. He had little time to eat or rest. Eventually, everyone deserted him and fled. The culmination of His mission would mean separation from His Heavenly Father and bearing the dark deeds of all history. His death would involve great suffering and the public spectacle of crucifixion. Yet, Jesus always chose to respond with courage.[1]

Despite His identity as the Son of God, Jesus rejected entitlement. He didn't buy into the temptation that He deserved unique perks or was due special treatment. Instead, He chose sacrifice. Despite being the King of kings, deserving of worship and honor, Jesus chose servanthood. Despite the temptation to seek His own ways, Jesus chose to submit to His Father's will in all things. Despite entering a temptation-filled world that focuses on self, Jesus chose to seek the Father's glory, purposes, and priorities.

BOTTOM LINE

When you find yourself on a difficult path as you follow Jesus, remember Jesus's radical and beautiful example. He's been in very difficult spaces. He can show you His way. Keep your eyes on Him. Know He understands. Know you are not alone. He is with you!

1. Steve Brown, *Jesus Centered* (Austin: Fedd Books, 2021), 72.

ACTION AND REFLECTION

Reflect on Jesus's example in the excerpt from Jesus Centered. How does what Jesus endured give you hope and courage today?

How does Jesus's example of sacrifice, servanthood, submission, and seeking the Father's glory influence how you follow Him?

PRAYER

(Inspired by Matthew 16:24 and Philippians 2:5–11)

> Dear Lord, by Your grace and in Your strength, I choose to deny myself, pick up my cross, and follow You today. Thank You for Your example, Jesus. Thank You for choosing sacrifice, servanthood, submission, and seeking the Father's glory above all else. Give me the courage to follow You, whatever the mission and whatever the cost. Keep my eyes on You always, but especially when I begin to lose heart and grow weary. I pray these things in the name of the One whose name is above all names.

3.

EXPECT TROUBLE

"In this world you will have trouble. But take
heart! I have overcome the world."
(John 16:33)

YEARS AGO, I had the privilege of visiting another country. I
didn't understand the language, and I needed to order lunch
from a menu that was incomprehensible to me. Thankfully, I'd
had pizza in the same restaurant the day before with someone fluent in the language, so I ordered what I thought was
the same pizza. However, when the smiling server returned
fifteen minutes later and put my plate down in front of me, I
was shocked by the smelly topping on my pizza. Apparently,
something was lost in translation because, as a non-fish lover,
I was now face-to-face with large and long sardines assem-
bled like the spokes of a wheel on my pizza.

I didn't expect a sardine pizza. I couldn't have imagined
the existence of a sardine pizza. Yet, I had apparently ordered,
and I certainly received, a sardine pizza.

Long story short, expectations matter. It can be surprising, disappointing, and even disorienting when you expect one
thing and get another. This holds true even beyond sardine
pizzas. When we expect life to be comfortable and it isn't, we
are likely to find ourselves in unexpected and uncharted terri-
tory when trouble hits.

Though we are bombarded with marketing campaigns seeking to shape our expectations toward a life of comfort and happiness, there's no guarantee. In fact, for Jesus's followers on this side of heaven, we can expect trouble. Jesus said as much in John 16:33: "In this world you will have trouble." Notice the word *will* that Jesus uses. It's an affirmative, concrete, expectant, and certain word. Jesus didn't use the word *might* or, like a weather forecaster, suggest there was a "good chance" of encountering trouble. According to Jesus, trouble is a given.

The roots that guarantee trouble go back to the garden of Eden. Our fallen and broken world means some degree of trouble for everyone. Everything and everyone has been tainted and corrupted. Trouble is brewing in the world around us. Trouble is even brewing inside us. Whether or not we are aware of it, trouble is also brewing in the spiritual realm.

Ironically, following Jesus can bring trouble. Jesus's path involved significant sacrifice, deep suffering, relentless opposition, and even brutal persecution. Foreshadowing the hardship his disciples could expect, Jesus said to his disciples, "The student is not above the teacher, nor a servant above his master" (Matthew 10:24). Faithfully following Jesus in this culture is in itself a recipe for trouble. But whatever trouble you face, the good news is that you aren't alone. Jesus is with you. And He's overcome the troubles of this world. He's also bigger than any trouble you face today or ever. He is your deliverer—from sin, from death, from fear, and from troubles.

It's also important to remember that today's trouble will pass. It is temporary. Ultimately, there is a day coming when troubles will be removed and gone forever. Jesus's return and reign will bring a day when "'He will wipe every tear from their eyes. There will be no more death' or mourning or crying or pain, for the old order of things has passed away" (Revelation 21:4).

BOTTOM LINE

If you are seeking to follow Jesus faithfully, don't be surprised by trouble. Instead, expect it. Know Jesus is with you. And Jesus changes everything. As J. R. R. Tolkien wrote, "The birth, death, and resurrection of Jesus mean that one day everything sad will come untrue."

ACTION AND REFLECTION

Take a few minutes and reflect on your expectations around trouble.

As a follower of Jesus, do you expect trouble in this life?

How does expecting trouble—even as a follower of Jesus—change how you endure trouble?

Does knowing that trouble is temporary and that Jesus is with you give you more courage?

PRAYER

(Inspired by 2 Corinthians 12:9 and John 16:33)

Lord Jesus, thank You for Your example of obedience and courage in the midst of troubles of all kinds. Though this world will have troubles, I take heart because You have overcome the world.

You are my strength, my helper, my guide, my deliverer, and my peace. I joyfully depend on You and trust You.

In and by Your strength, I choose to follow You.

If there's sacrifice required, in and by Your strength, I still choose to follow You.

If there's suffering to be endured, in and by Your strength, I still choose to follow You.

May Your presence and Your grace be sufficient to fill me with courage, and Your power be made perfect whenever I am weak!

I pray these things in the name of the One who has overcome the world.

4.

KEPT

To those who have been called, who are loved
in God the Father and kept for Jesus Christ.
(Jude 1)

MOVING IS A daunting process. After twenty years in the same
house, we decided to move across town. Over two decades,
we had accumulated a lot of stuff. So, before we packed, we
recognized that this was the time to discern and decide what
we were going to keep and what we were going to sell, give
away, or toss.

In the end, we only kept items that had special value or
were useful in the present or possibly the future. By keeping
items, we were making a decision to care for them, protect
them, and find a place for them in our future.

This same idea and intention of keeping comes up at the
beginning of Jude, a short twenty-five-verse letter just before
the book of Revelation. Though Jude is primarily a warning
against false teaching, the letter starts with these words, "To
those who have been called, who are loved in God the Father
and kept for Jesus Christ."

Reflecting on just this first verse in Jude gives courage.
For starters, if you are a Jesus follower, you have been called.
There's both intention and invitation in being called. You
were not left out or forgotten. And when you consider that

the creator of the universe, the all-powerful, all-knowing, and ever-present King of kings, is doing the calling, it is an incredible honor to be called.

Calling is for a purpose. God has called you, for His glory, to be about His purposes in this world. As my friend the best-selling author Mark Buchanan has said, "You are called to be holy menaces set loose on the face of this earth to be about the business of the King of kings." Be sure to note the modifying word "holy" ahead of the *menace*. Core to your calling is to be a disruptor for good who is set apart by and for God's work.

However, there's more to your calling than *doing*. As Os Guinness writes in *The Call*, "Our primary calling as followers of Christ is by him, to him, and for him. First and foremost, we are called to Someone (God), not to something (such as motherhood, politics, or teaching) or somewhere (such as the inner city or Outer Mongolia)."[2] In other words, at the core of your calling is *being* with God.

Back to Jude 1. This verse also declares that Jesus's followers are loved. The value of something is determined by what someone is willing to pay or give for it. To God the Father, you are worth His one and only Son, Jesus, who was given to rescue and redeem you. Knowing you are loved by God gives courage. No matter what situation you find yourself in, you have great value because God loves you. And just as you care for people and things you value, God is actively caring for you.

Beyond being called and loved, this verse says that Jesus's followers are kept. It makes sense that God would keep who He has intentionally called by invitation and who He clearly loves and greatly values. And just the way I kept items of value when I moved, God's keeping involves caring for, protecting, and finding a place for you in His future.

---

2. Os Guiness, *The Call* (Nashville: Word Publishing, 1998), 31.

There's also an important translation note around the word *kept* in this passage. While some translations say, "kept *for* Jesus Christ," others say, "kept *by* Jesus Christ," and others say, "kept *in* Jesus Christ." Each nuance is rich with meaning. If you are kept *for* Jesus Christ, you know you have incredible value and purpose. If you are kept *by* Jesus, then who or what can harm you when they have to first go through the Good Shepherd who is protecting and providing for you? If you are kept *in* Jesus, you are united with Jesus and live with the reality of His ongoing presence, His all-encompassing provision, and His eternal promises.

BOTTOM LINE

If you need more courage today, remember that you are called, loved, and ultimately kept by, for, and in Jesus. God has intentionally invited you to follow Him. You have a purpose. You are of great value to God and loved with a love that cannot be broken. Remember that Jesus, the Good Shepherd, is your protector and provider today.

ACTION AND REFLECTION

If you could only keep three things from your home (apart from people and pets), what would you keep? Why?

How does the truth that you are kept *by*, *for,* and *in* Jesus impact your perspective on your value to God and your circumstances?

PRAYER

(Inspired by Jude 1, Exodus 19:5 and Romans 8:38–39)

> Lord, by Your grace, You have called me. You
> have seen me, and you include me.

You call me first and foremost to Yourself, but you also call me to Your purposes for my life, for the world, and for Your glory.

By Your grace, You value me and call me Your treasured possession. You love me with a love I cannot fully fathom and a love that cannot be broken. By Your grace, You keep me.

You are actively involved in protecting and providing for me today and forever.

May Your personal calling, Your great love, and Your careful keeping fill me with courage today.

I pray these things in the name of my Savior and my keeper.

5.

WITH

"Surely, I am with you always, to the very end
of the age." (Matthew 28:20)

I HAVE A love/hate relationship with Christmas music. I get
uptight when I hear Christmas music in October. I cringe when
some songs are played over and over and over. I also get
slightly triggered whenever I hear "The Little Drummer Boy."
Back in grade six, my mind went blank while I was trying to
sing the first verse solo in front of my entire school. I ended
up repeating the only words I could remember: "Pa rum pum
pum pum." Without a doubt, that moment isn't my favorite
childhood memory.

Yet I love many of the old carols. One of my absolute favor-
ites is "O Come, O Come, Emmanuel." This carol is about a
people in the midst of great difficulty, deep darkness, and
even despair. They are calling on God to come, and at the end
of each verse, there is that repeated refrain: "Rejoice, rejoice"
in expectation that God will come. There's anticipation that
God's presence will change everything.

Jesus's arrival in this world—God with skin on—is the
answer to the prayerful cry behind this famous Christmas
carol. Emmanuel literally means "God with us," and the reality
of Emmanuel changes everything. In the moments and seasons of difficulty, darkness, and despair in your own life and

our world, you aren't abandoned or left on your own. God is present.

The theme of "God with us" is central to finding more courage. Here are just a few examples from Scripture:

> Where shall I go from your Spirit? Where can I flee from your presence? (Psalm 139:7)

> "Do not fear, for I am with you; do not be dismayed, for I am your God. I will strengthen you and help you; I will uphold you with my righteous right hand." (Isaiah 41:10)

> "Surely, I am with you always, to the very end of the age." (Matthew 28:20)

> "And I will ask the Father, and he will give you another advocate to help you and be with you forever – the Spirit of truth." (John 14:16-17)

> "Never will I leave you; never will I forsake you." (Hebrews 13:5)

The truth that God is with us goes beyond Jesus's physical presence in the world two thousand years ago. As a Jesus follower, God is with you today and every day until the very end of the age. This is a game-changing truth, especially if and when you find fears growing, resolve wavering, and strength depleting. God with you changes everything.

The incredible transformation of Peter in Acts is a stunning example. The Gospels record Peter's desertion and denials when Jesus was taken to be crucified. Yet in Acts 4, we see a radically different Peter. He's witnessed the resurrection, he's filled with the Holy Spirit, and he's found unwavering courage.

Brought before the powerful elders and teachers in Jerusalem to answer for his healing of a man lame from birth,

Peter doesn't back down under pressure. In fact, he doubles down. He boldly and courageously points to Jesus, who has been raised from the dead, as the man's healer. Despite facing grave punishment for pointing to and proclaiming Jesus, Peter continues and leaves no room for doubt in Acts 4:12: "Salvation is found in no one else, for there is no other name under heaven given to mankind by which we must be saved."

There was no way to miss Peter's bold courage. Nobody spoke to the religious leaders this way. So what was the key to Peter's courage? The answer was crystal clear. In fact, it was so clear that even the spiritually blinded religious leaders saw it. As Acts 4:13 says, "When they saw the courage of Peter and John and realized that they were unschooled, ordinary men, they were astonished, and they took note that these men had been with Jesus."

BOTTOM LINE

Peter and John had been *with* Jesus. Being *with* Jesus changes everything. Courage comes from knowing and trusting Jesus is *with* you. The best news is that Jesus is *with* you right now. He's *with* you next Tuesday at ten a.m. He's *with* you in your mountaintop moments. He's *with* you in your dark valleys. He's *with* you in desert seasons. He's with you when you face trials and opposition. May others be astonished when they see your courage, and may they take note that you have been *with* Jesus.

ACTION AND REFLECTION

Look up the words of "O Come, O Come, Emmanuel." Read the lyrics. Pray the lyrics.

Reflect on the difference Emmanuel—God with us—should make as you seek to find more courage. Try to identify five ways this truth impacts your day and your need for courage.

PRAYER

(Inspired by Acts 4:13)

Dear Lord, I am in awe that the prayer for Emmanuel was answered in history two thousand years ago. I am in awe that You are with me in my circumstances and challenges today. I am in awe that You are coming again to make all things right.

Remind me today that You are with me. Help me to be attentive to Your presence. I long to enjoy You today in my comings and goings.

I choose to put my challenges in perspective, knowing and trusting You are with me. I ask that You fill me with the courage that comes from being with You.

May others be astonished that I live differently because I have been with and I am with Jesus.

I pray these things in the name of Emmanuel, God with me.

6.

THE NOBODY LIES

> "Are not two sparrows sold for a penny? Yet
> not one of them will fall to the ground outside
> your Father's care. And even the very hairs
> of your head are all numbered. So don't be
> afraid; you are worth more than many spar-
> rows." (Matthew 10:29–31)

WHEN YOU ARE discouraged, challenged, and struggling, the
four "nobody lies" are never far away. The nobody lies are
subtle but powerful. Here they are:

1. Nobody sees me (I don't matter).
2. Nobody cares about me (I have no value).
3. Nobody understands me (I am alone).
4. Nobody can help me (I have no hope).

Once these lies get a foothold, they become toxic. When
they are left unaddressed, you can find yourself spiraling past
discouragement into despair.

In Mark 5, we meet a woman who must have struggled
with the nobody lies. She had been bleeding for twelve years.
Let me repeat: *twelve years*. Though she went to many doc-
tors, she only got worse. To add to her burden, she had spent
all her money on unhelpful medical treatments. To top things

off, she would have been deemed ceremonially unclean and unwelcome in community settings.

This kind of struggle is a breeding ground for the nobody lies. Yet this woman still holds out a glimmer of hope. She hears that Jesus is coming to town, and she thinks, "If I just touch his clothes, I will be healed" (Mark 5:28). So, she comes up behind Jesus, touches his cloak, and "immediately her bleeding stopped, and she felt in her body that she was freed from her suffering" (Mark 5:29).

At this point, Jesus realizes power has gone out from Him and asks the crowd, "Who touched my clothes?" (Mark 5:30). With people everywhere, His disciples find the question ridiculous and the answer impossible. Yet, in verse 32, we read, "But Jesus kept looking around to see who had done it." The woman then comes, falls trembling with fear at Jesus's feet, and tells Him what happened.

Jesus's response is moving and filled with both tenderness and encouragement. He says, "Daughter, your faith has healed you. Go in peace and be freed from your suffering." Imagine what it would have felt like for the woman to hear Jesus identify her with the intimacy, value, and belonging of "daughter." Notice, too, that Jesus turns the miracle back to the woman and her faith rather than pointing to His power.

This story strikes me on many levels. This woman is wonderfully desperate for Jesus, and her encounter with Jesus doesn't disappoint. If she was struggling with the nobody lies, her encounter with Jesus exposed and broke each lie: Jesus's presence, His power, and His words deposited courage in her.

BOTTOM LINE

If you are in a difficult moment or season, beware of the nobody lies. They are subtle. And they are toxic. Does anybody see you? Jesus does. Does anybody care about you?

Jesus does. Does anybody understand you? Jesus does. Can anybody help you? Jesus can.

ACTION AND REFLECTION

Review the "nobody lies":

> 1. Nobody sees me (I don't matter).
> 2. Nobody cares about me (I have no value).
> 3. Nobody understands me (I am alone).
> 4. Nobody can help me (I have no hope).

Are you more susceptible to any of these lies in certain life seasons or circumstances?

Do any of the lies resonate with your mindset right now?

If so, pray to reject each lie and declare the truth that Christ brings. Pray something like this: I reject the lie that nobody _____ me, and I declare that Jesus _____ me.

PRAYER

(Inspired by Psalm 95:6–7, Matthew 10:26–31, Ephesians 3:18, Psalm 139:1, Matthew 28:20, Psalm 121:2, and Psalm 62:5)

> Lord, my Maker: You are my God. I am Your child. You have the very number of hairs on my head numbered.
>
> You see me, know me, value me, and care for me.
>
> I can't even fathom how wide, high, long, and deep is Christ's love for me.
>
> You are greater than any challenge I can face. May these truths deposit courage in my heart and mind.
>
> I pray these things in the name of the One who is my helper and hope.

7.

JESUS THE ENCOURAGER

"Take courage! It is I. Do not be afraid."
(Matthew 14:27)

JESUS WAS AN incredible courage giver. Examples abound. James and John must have had more courage after Jesus gave them the name "Sons of Thunder" (Mark 3:13–17). The woman who had been bleeding for twelve years would have had more courage after Jesus healed her and turned the miracle back on her. "Take heart, daughter," Jesus said to her; "your faith has healed you" (Matthew 9:22).

Imagine Peter's response if you asked him to name his greatest earthly encourager. Peter would point to Jesus. He was the one who renamed him the "rock" (John 1:42) and called him out of the boat to walk on water with the words "Take courage! It is I. Do not be afraid" (Matthew 14:27). Jesus also encouraged Peter after his denials and desertion. On the shore of the Sea of Galilee, Peter received fresh courage when he was lovingly restored by his greatest encourager (John 21:1–19).

Rather than putting people down in order to make more of himself, Jesus called people up through his words and actions. Rather than dwelling on their shortcomings or failures, Jesus saw the potential and helped people find greater strength, resilience, and courage.

In following Jesus's example, we are called to be courage givers. What an incredibly meaningful compliment it would be for others to say they have more courage after spending time with you.

Almost everyone I talk to for long enough will reveal an area in their life in which they need more courage. If you focus on being a courage giver, you will never run short of opportunities to impact others positively. Few people long to spend more time with people who discourage them. People are drawn to courage givers. And courage givers end up being blessed themselves as they give courage to others.

Just as Jesus's words stirred courage, our words can give courage to others. You can start by pointing to God's character. Point to His presence, power, provision, and protection. Courage givers help stir more courage by painting a bigger, fuller, and clearer picture of God.

Your words can also point to God's faithfulness found in Scripture, in your own life, and in the life story of the person you are seeking to encourage. It is easy for all of us to forget or overlook God's faithfulness. Courage givers remember and remind others of God's incredible faithfulness and ongoing work.

Finally, your words can point to strengths, gifts, and positive qualities in others. Courage drains away when people focus on their failures, limitations, and negative self-talk. Courage givers point to the positive work God has done and continues to do in someone's life.

BOTTOM LINE

Jesus was an incredible encourager. Following His example, we are called to be courage givers to others. You can have an incredible impact by reminding others of God's character, faithfulness, and work.

ACTION AND REFLECTION

Here are three simple steps to follow Jesus's example as a courage giver:

1. Pray for the name of someone who might need encouragement.

2. When a specific person comes to mind, reach out by text, email, voice, or print to share an attribute of God or Scripture that might help fuel their courage.

3. Look over the list of Encouraging Words in Appendix II. With someone in mind, use the list to identify four to five words/characteristics that you see in them and can share to encourage them.

PRAYER

(Inspired by 1 Thessalonians 5:11)

Lord, Thank You for being a courage giver through Your example, Your words, and Your actions. I long to follow Your example and to be a courage giver to others.

Help me to be sensitive to others who may need courage in some area of their life. Fill me with such a big, clear, and full picture of who You are that it will overflow and help me point others to You. Help me remember Your faithfulness in my life and discern Your faithfulness in the lives of others so that I might point to Your faithfulness.

May everyone I spend time with leave me with more courage to press into Your calling and the next steps for their lives.

I pray these things in the name of my greatest earthly encourager, Jesus.

WEEK
TWO

8.

WHATEVER HAPPENS ...

I keep my eyes always on the LORD. With him at
my right hand, I will not be shaken. (Psalm 16:8)

I CAN THINK of a million things I'd rather do than wait in a doctor's office for important test results. The uncertainty can be incredibly sobering and nerve-wracking. Fears stir as your mind races with all the "what if" possibilities you've been trying not to google for days or weeks. You try to distract yourself by any means possible, but time seems to inch forward in very slow motion. If you've been there, you know exactly what I mean.

Just before COVID hit, my wife, Lea, was scheduled for a very important doctor's office visit. After a number of medical tests, all indications seemed to point to breast cancer, but there were still many unknowns. However, this was the day. In a few hours, we would sit in a doctor's office and officially hear the diagnosis and treatment options.

As I started the day, I was feeling very overwhelmed. To say that my courage quotient was low would be a big understatement. Thankfully, that morning, I came across a game-changing truth that has become one of my favorite go-to verses for finding more courage. The verse is Psalm 16:8. David writes, "I keep my eyes always on the LORD. With him at my right hand, I will not be shaken."

The first part of this verse calls us to refocus our eyes on the Lord. This is counterintuitive. Our default is to focus our eyes on the winds of uncertainty and the waves of turmoil around us. In our default posture, we end up sinking like Peter did when he started to walk on the water toward Jesus. With our eyes on the wind and waves, our courage drains, and fear consumes us.

The second half of the verse reminds us that we are not alone. If the Lord is at our right hand, then He is right there with us. And if our eyes are on the Lord, who is at our right hand, then our eyes are not looking ahead to what is in front of us. As we look at the Lord, He is able to look ahead at the wind and the waves. Our job is simply to look at Him. If we do, we will not be shaken. Everything changes when we keep our eyes on the Lord.

With our doctor's office visit a few hours away, Psalm 16:8 shifted my eyes away from the wind and waves and toward the Lord. With the Lord as my focus, peace began to overcome my uncertainty. Courage began to overcome my fear. And a prayer began to stir in my heart. This is the prayer I prayed:

Heavenly Father,

Whatever we learn today,
It doesn't catch You off guard;
It doesn't diminish Your love for us.

Whatever we learn today,
You are still bigger;
You are still in charge.

Whatever we learn today,
You can bring good from it and further
Your purposes.
You are with us and for us.

Whatever we learn today,
We continue to trust You.

Amen.

Later that day, we heard the words "You have cancer." It was surreal and hard news. But with our eyes on the Lord, we were not shaken. In the months ahead, there were tough moments when fears stirred, but we were not shaken.

Today, I am incredibly thankful for Lea's good health. I am also incredibly grateful for the truth of Psalm 16:8. I have memorized this verse. In fact, I also have a framed picture of the words on my office wall at work and another on the wall of our living room at home. I need to remember this truth every day: where we focus our eyes matters.

BOTTOM LINE

In moments when uncertainty stirs and fear begins to shake you, it's tempting to focus on the wind and waves of circumstances and challenges. The antidote, however, is to refocus your eyes on the Lord. Remember, He is at your right hand. Focusing on and trusting in His presence with you brings peace and courage.

ACTION AND REFLECTION

If you are facing uncertainty, consider praying a prayer similar to the one I prayed. I think it's a good prayer to pray any day. Here's a modified version focused on whatever happens today.

Heavenly Father,

Whatever happens today,
It doesn't catch You off guard;
It doesn't diminish Your love for me/us.

Whatever happens today,
You are still bigger;
You are still in charge.

Whatever happens today,
You can bring good from it and further Your purposes.
You are with me/us and for me/us.

Whatever happens today,
I/we continue to trust You.

Amen.

PRAYER

(Inspired by Romans 8:28 and Philippians 1:6)

Lord, thank You that I can have peace, knowing You are on Your throne and in charge today. Thank You that I can have peace, knowing that You love me more than I can fathom.

Thank You that I can have peace today, knowing that You are all-powerful. Thank You that I can have peace today, knowing that You are working out all things for my good and carrying Your plans for me on to completion until the day of Christ Jesus.

Thank You for being trustworthy.

By Your grace, keep my eyes focused on You and not the wind and waves around me.

I pray these things in the name of the One who is at my right hand.

9.

BE FAITHFUL

> The Lord is faithful, and he will strengthen you and protect you from the evil one. We have confidence in the Lord that you are doing and will continue to do the things we command. May the Lord direct your hearts into God's love and Christ's perseverance. (2 Thessalonians 3:3–5)

SOMETIMES WE CAN find ourselves in spaces where there isn't a quick fix. We can be in the proverbial tunnel and not see any light at the end of it. In these kinds of spaces, it's easy to feel powerless, and our minds can go down the road of worst-case scenarios. The uncertainty can be exhausting and lead to despair.

I found myself in one of these tunnels during my wife Lea's journey with breast cancer. The spoiler alert good news is that we made it through the tunnel and can celebrate her good health today. However, when we were in the tunnel, there wasn't a quick fix. Instead, there were months of difficult treatments and lots of uncertainty to navigate. To say the least, it was a daily grind—especially for my wife. And as a husband looking on, there were moments when I felt powerless and battled both fear and discouragement.

In the midst of this difficult journey, our Omega juicer taught me an important lesson. When the diagnosis was made, we jumped into learning everything we could to assist my wife's healing journey. Leveraging the powerful properties of raw vegetable concentrates was one discipline we adopted. Our juicer began to get a workout.

This discipline meant making fresh juice daily. It was easy at first. Fueled by the adrenaline from the crisis, I energetically sliced and diced vegetables for the juicer. Soon, each glass of fresh juice was being delivered with a sense of joy and hope that we would see a tangible difference in my wife's health.

However, as those early days of crisis turned into weeks and months of a chronic reality, my natural energy waned. On average, I would spend about half an hour every day slicing vegetables, feeding the juicer, unclogging the juicer, and cleaning up. Juicing wasn't convenient to my schedule. Some days, it was a chore. After a few weeks, taking the time to juice each day became harder and harder. I couldn't tell if the juice was making a real difference, and I began to wonder if I should just give up.

Can you relate? Does our journey with juicing resonate with your journey through a difficult time? Have you ever found yourself in a crisis or tackling an unexpected challenge? Maybe you experienced an initial energy boost fueled by adrenaline that dwindled over time.

When the early days of crisis turn into a chronic reality—with no end in sight—you can begin to feel the effects of the grind. In the grind, your energy and hope start to decline. You feel short on joy and long on burden. You begin to wonder if what you are doing is actually making a difference. You quietly lose courage and wrestle with giving up.

Let me point you toward the lesson my Omega juicer taught me—the value and power of everyday faithfulness.

As I faithfully did my daily work with the juicer, I learned that the benefit of juicing wasn't my enjoyment. It wasn't about how it made me feel or how much impact I could see or measure. The thirty minutes a day was actually about seeking to faithfully and practically express love for my wife. I also discovered that my daily juicing discipline was a simple expression of faithfulness to God. Strangely enough, during the faithful practice of juicing, I found myself worshipping God and being reminded of His faithfulness.

When you are faithful, God sees your faithfulness and delights in it. Thankfully, you don't need to drum up faithfulness on your own. While faithfulness is a choice and a commitment to persevere, faithfulness is ultimately a fruit of the Spirit. Its source flows from the unquenchable resources of our faithful God.

BOTTOM LINE

In long tunnels of challenge, your best response may be to simply practice daily faithfulness. Let your faithfulness become an act of worship, no matter the outcome. May your faithfulness remind you of God's faithfulness.

ACTION AND REFLECTION

In the midst of a challenge you are facing, is there a regular discipline that you are already practicing? If so, seek to reframe this discipline as an act of faithfulness and love toward God and/or others. This reframing is a mindset. It's also a prayer. As you engage in this practice, pray something like, "Faithful God, I am not in control. I can't fix this situation on my own. But I do seek to be faithful even by doing little things like _____. Please receive my faithfulness as an act of love toward You, and _____. I entrust the outcomes to Your good care."

PRAYER

(Inspired by 2 Thessalonians 1:3–5 and Lamentations 3:22–23)

Faithful God, because of Your great love, I am not consumed. Your compassion never fails. Great is your faithfulness.

Though I may feel like I am in a tunnel, please strengthen and give me courage.

Protect me from discouragement and despair.

Direct my heart deeper into Christ's love, and grant me Christ's perseverance.

Though my power to fix or change things is so limited, I trust in Your faithfulness and Your power.

By Your grace, guide me and teach me to be faithful in big and small ways.

Whatever happens, may You receive my faithfulness as an act of love to You and toward others.

I pray these things in the name of the Faithful One.

10.

GOD SEES YOU

> She [Hagar] gave this name to the LORD who spoke to her: "You are the God who sees me," for she said, "I have now seen the One who sees me." (Genesis 16:13)

AFTER A QUIET day of reflection, it was time for me to make my way to an important meeting near the airport. So I used my Uber app to book a ride and waited for my driver, Darren, to arrive.

When his car pulled up, and I jumped in the backseat, I immediately heard Christian music playing. This was unusual, but it opened the door to conversation, so I asked Darren if he was a man of faith. He answered that he was and asked if I was. I said yes, and then Darren asked if, by any chance, I was a pastor. When I said yes, he loudly responded, "No way."

From there, Darren poured out his life story. He said that he had been driving around all day talking to God about how he had been struggling to follow Him. He said it was like he would take two steps forward in his relationship with God and then three back. His marriage was in trouble, and his wife was at counseling as we were driving to the airport.

To summarize, Darren had been driving around all day wondering if God saw or heard him—and then I got in his car. Since it seemed like not a small miracle that God would put a pastor in his backseat, he asked if I would pray for him when we got to my airport hotel. I gave an immediate yes. To me, it totally seemed like God had somehow penetrated Uber's booking software to get me in the back of Darren's car with a tangible reminder that God sees him.

By the time we parked at my hotel, I was more than ready to pray. By then, I had recalled several instances in Scripture where God saw people who thought they were alone and forgotten. I remembered Genesis 16 and a mistreated and pregnant Hagar wandering around without any hope, only to be reminded that God sees her. I remembered Luke 19 and an unpopular tax collector named Zacchaeus being astonished that while surrounded by crowds, Jesus saw him up in a tree and called him by name.

Long story short, I prayed and thanked God for seeing Darren in his Uber car. I thanked God for matching our Uber ride to remind Darren that He sees him just like Jesus saw Zacchaeus up in the tree and just like God saw pregnant and despairing Hagar alone in the desert.

My heart felt full when I landed at "Amen." I could tell Darren was deeply moved, and then, to my surprise, he asked if he could pray for me. After he prayed, we fist-bumped, and then I made my way into the hotel. While I was waiting in line for my key, I felt a tap-tap-tap in my spirit. Then I sensed this question, "Steve, what were you doing right before Darren picked you up?" I thought back and remembered that I was writing in my journal. Then I sensed the question, "What were you writing in your journal?" I fished my journal out of my bag and read my last entry. It read something like, "God, I feel tired, alone, and overwhelmed. Would you reveal Yourself in some way to me today?"

At this point, some important and incredible dots were connected. Up until that moment, I thought that being in Darren's Uber was all about God seeing him. But now, as I reflected on

Darren praying for me, it seemed like God had just done a two-for-one miracle. He hadn't just reminded Darren that He sees him. God had also reminded me that He sees me.

It can be easy to remind other people that God sees them. We can believe it. However, it gets much harder to acknowledge that God sees us. Somehow, this truth that we are quick to remind others of becomes blurry in our circumstances and challenges.

That day, through an Uber ride, I was reminded that God does see me. This was a day changer for me. I was reminded in an unforgettable way that I'm in God's view 24/7/365. I'm not alone or overlooked ever. Talk about a fresh injection of courage!

BOTTOM LINE

If you are in a difficult moment or season, there's news that can give you the courage to press on: God sees you. You matter to Him. You are not alone.

ACTION AND REFLECTION

Read Genesis 16. Imagine what Hagar must have been feeling. She had been mistreated to the point that she had to leave the provision and protection of her master's household. She was pregnant, she was alone, and she had no way to earn money or protect herself. Leaving was close to an act of suicide. Yet, God saw her, and that knowledge changed everything. How does the reality that God sees you change your perspective?

PRAYER

(Inspired by Genesis 16 and Psalm 139)

> God, You are the God who sees me. You watch over me because I matter to You.

STEVE A. BROWN

Thank You that I am never unnoticed. Just like Your eyes saw my unformed body as You created my inmost being, You watch over my comings and goings every day. Your Spirit is always with me.

Thank You that I am never alone. You hem me in behind and before. Such knowledge is too lofty for me to understand fully.

Guard me from any lies that I might be tempted to embrace when I am alone or feeling overwhelmed.

May being under Your watchful and present care 24/7/365 give me fresh courage for whatever comes.

I pray this in the name of the God who sees me.

11.

BREATHE

Be still, and know that I am God. (Psalm 46:10)

I WAS STRESSED out and overwhelmed. In that particular season of life, the combination of the intensity of parenting young kids and the complexity of leadership at work felt more than daunting. I didn't know what to do, but I did know I needed some perspective. So I called a trusted mentor. I asked Evon, then in his early nineties, if he remembered the feelings of stress and anxiety when he was my age.

Despite his clear mind and strong memory, Evon responded that he actually didn't remember those kinds of feelings and struggles from back when he was my age.

Evon's answer more than surprised me. It was also exactly what I needed to hear. I began to recognize that maybe the things I was so concerned about in the here and now of the present might not even be part of my memory later in life. So I said to myself, *If this is something that you're likely not even going to remember down the road, then why are you so consumed with it now? Breathe. It's going to be okay. This moment is simply a moment. It's not permanent. This too shall pass.*

Beyond Evon's sage wisdom from a long life well-lived, there is also much biblical wisdom that calls us to pause and breathe in the midst of life's sometimes overwhelming intensity, pressures, and complexity. We are called to remember and refocus on who God is. This is the focus of Psalm 46. It starts: "God is our refuge and strength, an ever-present help in trouble. Therefore we will not fear, though the earth give way and the mountains fall into the heart of the sea, though its waters roar and foam and the mountains quake with their surging."

The refrain repeated in verses 7 and 11 continues, "The LORD Almighty is with us; the God of Jacob is our fortress."

The capstone is verse 10: "Be still, and know that I am God."

Can you relate to moments of trouble and fear when it feels like the earth has given way? Has your life ever felt like immovable mountains falling into the sea and waters roaring around you? Verse 10 tells you to breathe. This isn't a self-help trick but an act of your will to refocus on the incredible and unchanging character of God.

According to Psalm 46, God is your refuge. In other words, He's your safe place. He's also your strength. If you don't have strength on your own for today, the good news is that God's strength is available to you. To add to the good news, God isn't absent; He's an ever-present help in trouble. He is with you. He's your fortress, and He is your protector.

BOTTOM LINE

Don't be consumed by your present circumstances. Remember, this moment will pass. Remember and rest in God's character. Be still. Focus on Him. Breathe.

ACTION AND REFLECTION

Slowly read Psalm 46. Pause and take three deep breaths after verse 7 and then again after verse 11. Reread and repeat two more times.

PRAYER

(Inspired by Psalm 46)

God, You are my refuge and strength, an ever-present help in trouble. Therefore, I will not fear, though the earth gives way and the mountains fall into the heart of the sea.

For You are the Lord Almighty, who is with me. You are my fortress.

I choose to turn my eyes from my circumstances and focus them on You.

For You are the Lord Almighty, who is with me. You are my fortress.

I choose to be still and to know that You are God.

For You are the Lord Almighty, who is with me. You are my fortress.

I breathe deeply and slowly.

For You are the Lord Almighty, who is with me. You are my fortress.

I pray this in the name of the only One whose name will be exalted among the nations and in the earth.

12.

VICTORY RESTS WITH THE LORD

The horse is made ready for the day of battle,
but victory rests with the LORD. (Proverbs 21:31)

I SOMETIMES REREAD my old journals. Here is an excerpt from one entry: "After Tuesday night's deflating, confusing, and frustrating meeting, I returned home very weary and emotionally fragile. Before heading to bed, I looked at each of the kids. They were sleeping soundly, seemingly without a care in the world, and fully at peace under their parents' care. I tossed and turned through the night. After tossing and turning until morning, I asked myself: The kids are at peace under our care—how come I'm not at peace under God's care?"

At the heart of this question is a core biblical theme— trust. Unfortunately, I'm often too slow to trust God. Instead, I choose to push ahead in my own strength and on my own timeline. My super hard work to keep things moving forward can be a camouflage for my own unbelief and fear. I've discovered this approach doesn't breed more courage. Instead, I'm left with stress, fatigue, and an overwhelming sense that everything rests with me.

Proverbs 21:31 is one of my favorite verses on trust: "The horse is made ready for the day of battle, but victory rests with the LORD." It's important to note that the verse points to a battle. The natural context seems to be a military battle, but there are also spiritual battles, mental battles, fear battles, and more.

Whatever type of battle you face, the first half of the verse implies there are some things to do in order to get the horses ready for battle. For example, if King Solomon turned to you and told you to make ready the horses for battle, you would have your work cut out for you. You would need to ready thousands of horses. When you factor in everything from feeding to transporting to training to outfitting, you would need a strategy, detailed plans, diligence, discipline, and readiness to do lots of hard work.

Yet despite bringing your best to all the necessary work, victory isn't guaranteed. Pay attention to the really important comma in this verse. The comma separates what you faithfully bring to the equation in the first half of the verse from what only God can bring. The second half of the verse is a reminder that only God can bring victory.

There is freedom in the truth that victory ultimately rests with the Lord. You are ultimately and utterly dependent on God. Whatever situation you find yourself in, victory isn't all on you. You do need to be faithful and do your best, but you cannot control outcomes or timelines. You cannot get to victory on your own. God is in charge.

So rather than frantically pressing forward in your own strength and trying to carry the weight of the outcome, your posture needs to be one of dependence, surrender, and trust in the Lord. Trusting God is a choice and an act of obedience. Trusting God is for our good. Trusting God brings courage.

BOTTOM LINE

If you are in a battle, victory isn't all on you. You can and need to do your part and prepare the horses for battle, but your trust ultimately needs to be *in the Lord.* Only in trusting Him can you find deep peace and enduring hope in the midst of the battle. Only by trusting Him can you find persevering courage to face the battle.

ACTION AND REFLECTION

Reflect and pray—Are you carrying any burdens that you shouldn't? Where are you trying to make a way rather than trust God's way? If anything comes to mind, take a moment to confess your independence, unbelief, and fears. Then choose to give and trust this area to the Lord's able care by praying: "God, I choose to trust You with _____."

PRAYER

(Inspired by Proverbs 21:30–31 and John 15:5)

> Faithful God, I declare Proverbs 21:30, "There is no wisdom, no insight, no plan that can succeed against the LORD." Your plans and Your purposes will ultimately prevail.
>
> While You invite me to ready the horses and faithfully do my part, I am ultimately and utterly dependent on You. You are mighty. You are able.
>
> Forgive me for living and striving as if victory rests with me. I can do nothing apart from You. You are my strength, my helper, my provider, my protector, and my victory. I choose to trust You today.
>
> I choose to trust You with _____.
>
> I pray this in the name of my trustworthy and victorious Lord.

13.

NONANXIOUS PRESENCE

I am the LORD your God who takes hold of
your right hand and says to you, Do not fear;
I will help you. (Isaiah 41:13)

FERRIES ARE PART of the highway system where I live. Every day, ferries are moving thousands of people and vehicles back and forth between islands and to and from the mainland. Some people take ferries to work or school every single day. Others use ferries to visit beautiful island settings for vacations or to visit friends and family.

The vast majority of ferry trips are uneventful. However, I recall one disastrous trip. It was a Friday of a very busy long weekend. The *Queen of Oak Bay*, a 450-foot ferry, was carrying 544 passengers, 36 crew, and 76 vehicles. It was beginning its final approach to the docking terminal at Horseshoe Bay, just outside Vancouver. Everything seemed normal until the engine was needed to slow the forward momentum of the large ferry. For some reason, there was no engine power. Without engine power, there was no way to slow or stop the ferry. The ferry was going to crash.

With no ideal alternatives, the captain pointed the ship toward the small marina beside the ferry terminal. Passengers were warned of an imminent impact, and the ship's whistle was sounded repeatedly in hopes of clearing people off the boats and docks at the marina. The ship steered into the marina and eventually ran aground after damaging twenty-eight sailboats and many docks. Thankfully and mercifully, no one was hurt on shore or the ferry.

In the midst of a crisis or unexpected challenge, it's understandable that fear might stir and even paralyze. It's also reasonable for fear to become contagious from one person to another. However, that day, the passengers on the *Queen of Oak Bay* would have been hoping—even expecting—that the captain would exercise steady courage in those critical moments. They needed the captain to be a nonanxious presence who would make the best decisions possible and be a calm example to the rest of the crew and passengers.

Being a nonanxious presence is a critical trait and practice when you are responsible for others. It's also critical for anyone facing a challenge. If your spirit is settled, steady, and filled with peace, then you will think more clearly and act more courageously. Your example will also help those around you be more steady, settled, and courageous.

The opposites are also true. If you are anxious, you won't think your best, be your best, or be as courageous. Your fear can also become contagious and negatively impact others.

While years of training and experience may have helped to ground and steady the captain of *Queen of Oak Bay*, Jesus-followers have a special source of courage. Our courage comes from who God is, what He's already done, and what He promises for the future. It takes more than a lifetime to unpack the wonder and magnitude of who God is. For a start, He's faithful; He's all-powerful and bigger than any challenge you can face. He's also your peace. And because of the cross—what He's already done—you are secure in Christ both now and forevermore. Nothing and no one can mess with that truth.

BOTTOM LINE

God promises to be with you as your helper today. Isaiah 41:13 is a beautiful reminder, "I am the LORD your God who takes hold of your right hand and says to you, Do not fear; I will help you." You are not alone. He is with you. He is the Lord your God. Whatever you are going through, He's got you. He's bigger. He's your peace. He will help you.

ACTION AND REFLECTION

Try to personalize and memorize Isaiah 41:13. Here's a personalized version:

> The LORD my God takes hold of my right hand. He says to me, "Do not fear, [insert your name]; I will help you.

As you recite, memorize, and pray this personalized verse, try holding out your right hand to physically acknowledge that God is with you.

PRAYER

(Inspired by Psalm 3 and Psalm 56:3)

> Lord, thank You that You never tremble with fear.
>
> From Your throne, You are ultimately in charge. You laugh and scoff at those who oppose You and Your purposes. Your purposes will ultimately prevail.

You are strong and mighty. You are my strong foundation and my shield. You are my refuge and my strong tower.

You are present as my helper. Thank You that I can trust You. Following King David's example, when I am afraid, I put my trust in You.

I pray this in the name of the One who is my peace.

14.

COME ALONGSIDE

One who has unreliable friends soon comes to ruin, but there is a friend who sticks closer than a brother. (Proverbs 18:24)

IT'S AN UNFORGETTABLE Olympic moment. At the 1992 Summer Olympics in Barcelona, Great Britain's Derek Redmond advanced to the 400-meter semifinal. It had been four long years since an Achilles injury forced him to pull out at the last minute from his heat at the Seoul Olympics. He endured multiple operations in his recovery and battled back to be part of the 1991 World Championship 4x400 team. So, after logging the fastest time in the first round and winning his quarterfinal heat, this Olympics seemed like his moment.

The starter's pistol went off, and Redmond started strong, but 250 yards from the finish, he pulled up in agony. His hamstring had torn. Redmond initially went down but somehow stood up and began to limp toward the finish. His face expressed both the physical pain and emotional anguish of the moment, but he kept hobbling forward.

Adding to the unfolding drama, Redmond's father, Jim, jumped onto the track. Redmond's dad, beautifully demonstrating a father's love, pushed past security to get to his son's side on the track. Derek clung to his dad's shoulder for support, and they continued step-by-step toward the finish.

Though the race was long over for all the other competitors, Redmond's courageous perseverance captured the attention of the entire stadium. The crowd of 65,000 were on their feet cheering as Derek Redmond, in agonizing pain, finally crossed the finish line. Longtime Olympic commentator Brian Williams was nearly speechless and summarized this powerful moment with the words, "That is the Olympic spirit."

Without a doubt, Derek Redmond's story beautifully illustrates the ideals of the Olympics. However, it also demonstrates the spirit of the church. When we see someone struggling in their race of life, we are to take on the role of courage giver and come alongside. This is what "Carry each other's burdens" (Galatians 6:2) is all about. And like the cheering crowd of 65,000, the body of Christ needs to be giving courage to one another.

BOTTOM LINE

As the church, we are called to be "for" the burdened, the brokenhearted, the fearful, and the challenged. In other words, we are called to come alongside and be courage givers. That's the true spirit of the church.

ACTION AND REFLECTION

Pause and pray. Is there anyone in your life or sphere of influence who is facing an unexpected setback or trial?

Can you think of someone who is navigating a challenge that has become a long-term journey?

Take a moment to pray for them right now.

Then reach out to them in some way—a text, an email, a call, a visit, a bouquet of flowers, a meal, a gift card—to remind them that you are walking with them and cheering them on. You don't need perfect words to give courage. Pray, show up, reach out, be present, and walk alongside.

PRAYER

(Inspired by Proverbs 18:24, Isaiah 41:10, Galatians 6:2, and Hebrews 13:6)

> Lord, thank You for being present with me in my hardest miles and moments. You are a friend who sticks closer than a brother. You have come alongside me to strengthen me, help me, and uphold me.
>
> Thank You, too, for the courage givers who have come alongside me to help bear my burdens when I have felt alone or overwhelmed. I specifically thank You for _____.
>
> Thank You, too, for giving me the role of being a courage giver for others. Help me to be attentive to unexpected moments today where someone might need courage, and help me be faithful as a courage giver to those who I know are in difficult places.
>
> I pray these things in the name of the One who is my helper.

WEEK
THREE

15.

OVERCOMING FEAR

Some trust in chariots and some in horses,
but we trust in the name of the LORD our God.
(Psalm 20:7)

FEAR COMES IN all shapes and sizes. Fear of heights, public speaking, snakes, spiders, the dark, flying, and dying are all common fears. We can relate to the feeling, power, and impact of fear. It's a very common theme in the Bible. Most of the "big names" in God's story struggled with fear. Even unstoppable Paul, the great and bold missionary, wrote about "conflicts on the outside, fears within" (2 Corinthians 7:5).

But not all fears are equal. There is a spectrum of fear. On one end of the spectrum, there is fear that is like a warning light. It makes you aware that all may not be right. It calls you to pay attention. You might experience this kind of fear when you wait in line to bungee jump off a crazy high bridge, when you are tempted to make a very wrong choice, or when you are facing an unexpected or new situation. Interestingly, this kind of warning-light fear can sometimes also stir people to unexpected energy or even acts of heroism.

On the other end of the fear spectrum is a type of fear that can take control of or paralyze us. This kind of fear has a variety of symptoms, from constant worry to frenetic activity, workaholism, and escapism. Ultimately, this kind of fear squelches courage.

Let me share a personal example. I was feeling worn down and anxious. In truth, I had been feeling this way for some time. It had been a challenging season. I knew that some of the feelings were simply a result of the fatigue that comes from nonstop pressure, challenge, and hard work. However, as I reread my journal from the past year, I recognized that these feelings had become an ongoing, consistent pattern.

I was tired of feeling this way, and I sensed something was wrong. I longed for Jesus's words in Matthew 11:28, "Come to me, all you who are weary and burdened, and I will give you rest." Unfortunately, my soul was not at rest, and my yoke didn't seem easy, nor was my burden light.

So I invited a wise spiritual mentor into my inner struggle. After I shared what I was feeling and the ongoing pattern of fatigue, pressure, and worry, my mentor asked me a simple question. He asked, "Where does trust fit into all this?"

I'm not sure how I initially responded, but I know that I was angry. In my mind, my mentor didn't seem to understand how hard I was working, how I was giving everything I had, plus some. It seemed that my mentor wanted me to do even more by trusting God more.

After our conversation, his question continued to stir in me. That evening, I spent some time reflecting on my trust in God. There was no doubt that I was working hard. Hard work was required. But was I really trusting God? My honest answer was no.

In truth, my hard work ethic wasn't about God's glory. My driven workaholism was actually a thinly veiled cover for my fear. My particular brand of fear was the fear of failure.

My deep-seated belief was if this endeavor failed, I would be letting down God and many others. To avoid this, I had determined to avoid failure at all costs.

In practical terms, avoiding failure meant working in my own strength and getting close to the point of exhaustion. In my mission to avoid failure, I wasn't trusting God. Courage had been replaced by the slave driver of fear.

In response, I confessed my independence and fear to God. I also chose to trust God in whatever happened—success or failure—and surrendered the challenges to Him. When I awoke the next morning, I was still tired from too many hours of work. But I had a new peace. I trusted God, and I was no longer ruled by fear.

BOTTOM LINE

Fear is common. It can be an important data point to pay attention to, but it shouldn't be your master. It can be a slave driver that zaps courage. Jesus's followers shouldn't be ruled by fear. Instead, we are called to choose to trust God.

ACTION AND REFLECTION

Try to identify any specific fears that are driving or controlling you. Fear of failure, fear of rejection, fear of people, fear of the cost, fear of change, and fear of success are a few to consider.

Simply identifying and naming your fears brings them into the light and breaks some of their power.

Confess the specific fear(s) or unbelief to God, and ask for forgiveness where fear has replaced trust and taken control. Then, by God's grace, choose to trust God in that specific area—i.e., "God, I confess and turn from the fear of _____, and by Your strength, I choose to trust You with _____." Pray the aspect of God's character that counters the fear.

PRAYER

(Inspired by Psalms 20 and 56, and Mark Buchanan)

> Trustworthy God, I don't trust in modern-day chariots or horses. I choose to trust in You. I reject my fear of _____, and I declare that You are my protector and my provider. You are my peace. My courage is found in You.
>
> I command that the fear(s) of _____ leave me and invite the peace of God to fill me.
>
> I pray this in the name of the Lord my God.

16.

GET SOME SLEEP

The LORD is my shepherd, I lack nothing.
He makes me lie down in green pastures,
he leads me beside quiet waters,
he refreshes my soul. (Psalm 23:1–2)

I BELIEVE THERE'S a correlation between physical stamina and courage. For instance, when I'm not well rested, my fears seem to magnify and multiply. My thinking gets cloudy, my resolve diminishes, I become more sensitive to criticism, my fuse toward anger is shorter, and my susceptibility to fear and negative thinking increases.

Sleep is foundational to physical stamina and, by extension, to courage. Endless studies powerfully demonstrate that our sleep, both in quality and quantity, is incredibly important to our physical stamina, health, and everyday effectiveness. There are also endless studies that point to an epidemic of sleeplessness. As a result, many people are navigating the challenges of life with less stamina and courage than they could.

You can see the need for and power of rest in the prophet Elijah's life. In his spectacular showdown with the prophets of Baal, God demonstrated His power by miraculously burning up Elijah's sacrifice and turning the people toward God and away from the prophets of Baal. Elijah followed up this show-down by running ahead of Ahab all the way to Jezreel—close to a marathon distance.

Then, when Elijah heard about Jezebel's pledge to have him killed, his courage was drained, and he "was afraid and ran for his life" (1 Kings 19:3). Completely physically depleted, Elijah declared, "I have had enough, Lᴏʀᴅ," and asked that God would take his life. Then he slept. After sleep, food, and a touch from an angel of the Lord, Elijah was rejuvenated and continued his journey over forty days and forty nights to Horeb.

A more contemporary example that links rest and courage is found in the life of Winston Churchill. Churchill was a prolific napper. His naps were part of his daily regimen, especially as he led Great Britain during World War II. As Churchill said:

> You must sleep sometime between lunch and dinner, and no halfway measures .... Don't think you will be doing less work because you sleep during the day. That's a foolish notion held by people who have no imagination. You will accomplish more. You get two days in one—well, at least one and a half, I'm sure. When the war started, I had to sleep during the day because that was the only way I could cope with my responsibilities.[3]

While there are many practical tips and helpful techniques to help us sleep, we shouldn't forget that there are also some important spiritual realities:

- First, we are designed by God to require sleep.

3. Jim Loehr and Tony Schwartz, *The Power of Full Engagement* (New York: The Free Press, 2003), 61.

- Second, sleep is a reminder that we are not God. We cannot do it all, but God doesn't need to slumber or sleep (Psalm 121:4). We need sleep. In many ways, sleeping is a spiritual discipline.

- Third, when we sleep, we are forced to relinquish control. In this act, we have the opportunity to choose to trust God to watch over all the pieces of our lives. As David wrote in Psalm 4:8, "In peace I will lie down and sleep, for you alone, LORD, make me dwell in safety."

BOTTOM LINE

As you seek to walk with courage, how is your physical stamina? Are you physically worn out? Exhausted? Are your fears getting magnified and multiplied? Is your thinking getting cloudy, or are your emotions getting fragile? The best thing you can do—and even the most spiritual response—might be to follow the example of Elijah and Winston Churchill and get some rest. Take a nap. Sleep.

ACTION AND REFLECTION

To help you with the spiritual side of sleep, reflect on these three questions to clear your head and heart before sleep:

What are you thankful for? Start back at the beginning of your day. When were you blessed? Sometimes, these blessings are big and unforgettable. But also look for blessings in the ordinary everyday things and even in difficult moments. Keep searching until you find at least three things you are thankful for from the day. Then thank God. This simple act of thanksgiving can positively change your heart and mind as you get set for rest.

Is forgiveness needed? Taking guilt, shame, anger, or hurt into your sleep won't help your rest. Psalm 139:23–24 reads, "Search me, God, and know my heart; test me and know my anxious thoughts. See if there is any offensive way in me, and lead me in the way everlasting." Pray this simple prayer, reflect on your day, and confess anything to God if/ when you identify any offensive ways. As you seek forgiveness for yourself, by God's grace, you can also extend forgiveness to those who have trespassed against you.

What do you need to entrust to God? Are you carrying some emotional, mental, or practical burdens from the day? Are there some people, situations, circumstances, or unfinished business that you need to entrust to God? Taking this weight into the night, even subconsciously, will hinder your rest. Instead, pray a simple prayer like "God, I choose to trust _____ into Your good care this night."

PRAYER

(Inspired by Psalms 4, 23, and 121)

> My Good Shepherd, You do not slumber nor sleep. You are filled with strength and power 24/7/365. I confess that I am not. I need rest. I pray for the grace of sleep and deep rest.
>
> I choose to entrust my worries, fears, and burdens to You and Your good care. I choose to surrender and rest in sleep. May my sleep help fuel courage so that I might be faithful in Your purposes for my day. I pray these things in the name of the Good Shepherd who watches over me and continues to move

forward His purposes in my life and the world
even as I sleep.

Another helpful and beautiful night prayer from *A New Zealand Prayer Book* was given to me by a friend. I've shortened and slightly modified it.

Lord, it is the night after a long day;
what has been done has been done,
what has not been done has not been done.
I entrust all to You.

17.

LAMENT

How long, LORD? Will you forget me forever?
How long will you hide your face from me?
How long must I wrestle with my thoughts
and day after day have sorrow in my heart?
How long will my enemies triumph over me?
(Psalm 13:1–2)

SOMETIMES, WHEN I'M reading through certain Psalms, I find myself asking, "Can you really talk that way to God?" It's usually David who is calling out, crying out, and questioning God in these psalms. His words are raw and real and often filled with desperation. David's courage tank is on fumes.

There's actually a name given to this kind of crying-out prayer—lament. Lament is a heart cry of frustrations, sorrow, questions, and grief. Laments are raw and real prayers. They lay out the pain, troubling situations, and disappointments of our broken lives, our difficult challenges, and this broken world before God.

Laments often ask God why. For instance, Psalm 10 starts with, "Why, LORD, do you stand far off? Why do you hide yourself in times of trouble?" On the cross, Jesus quotes Psalm 22, "My God, my God, why have you forsaken me?"

Laments also often ask God how long. Psalm 13 starts, "How long, LORD? Will you forget me forever? How long will you hide your face from me?" If you are in or have been in a difficult space, these why and how long questions have likely been questions you've asked or wanted to ask God.

About a third of the 150 Psalms have themes of lament. Of course, there's also an entire book in the Old Testament called Lamentations. Job, Jeremiah, and Jesus also lamented. Laments don't hold back feelings from God. After all, God already knows. He's big enough to hear heart cries. And rather than being offensive to God, voicing our deepest thoughts and feelings seems to result in a deeper intimacy with God.

Take a look at Psalm 13. It's a Psalm of lament that follows a pattern. Verses 1 and 2 are heart cries to God: "How long, LORD? Will you forget me forever? How long will you hide your face from me? How long must I wrestle with my thoughts and day after day have sorrow in my heart? How long will my enemies triumph over me?"

Verses 3 and 4 are calls for God's help: "Look on me and answer, LORD my God. Give light to my eyes, or I will sleep in death, and my enemies will say, 'I have overcome him,' and my foes will rejoice when I fall."

Verses 5 and 6 are an affirmation of who God is (even though verses 1 and 2 are still very raw and real): "But I trust in your unfailing love; my heart rejoices in your salvation. I will sing the LORD's praise, for he has been good to me."

BOTTOM LINE

If you find yourself in the midst of crisis, change, chaos, or challenge, you will need to find more courage. However, finding more courage doesn't mean wallpapering over your grief, disappointments, or questions and pretending they aren't there. The path to finding more courage and deeper intimacy with God often passes through the valley of lament.

ACTION AND REFLECTION

Write your own Psalm of lament following the same pattern as Psalm 13. You can pour out your heart to God in your words, or you can write/say a prayer, a prayer of lament, using these prompts:

> Lord, these things have been hard ... (list what's been hard and why).
>
> Lord, in the midst of what I'm going through, I need Your help. Would You help ...? (list where and what you need help with).
>
> Lord, I choose to trust You regardless of what's happened/happening. You are ... (declare truth about God's character).

PRAYER

(Inspired by Ephesians 3:12 and Revelation 21:4)

> Lord, I'm thankful because of Christ that I can approach You with boldness, freedom, and confidence—especially when I am over-whelmed, disappointed, discouraged, filled with hard questions, frustrated, or even angry. Thank You for being big enough, strong enough, and grace-filled enough to allow me to be real and raw in my heart's cries.
>
> Thank You for loving, caring, and listening to me—especially when I don't understand or even misunderstand You.
>
> In each step and chapter of this journey, I want to turn toward You, not away from You.

Please guard my heart and mind. Draw me deeper into my relationship with You.

Please protect me when I'm most vulnerable. Remind me of Your presence with me. Fill me with the courage to press on.

I pray these things in the name of the One who "'will wipe every tear from their eyes. There will be no more death' or mourning or crying or pain, for the old order of things has passed away" (Revelation 21:4).

18.

GROW YOUR VISION

LORD, our Lord, how majestic is your name in all the earth! You have set your glory in the heavens. (Psalm 8:1)

I USED TO pride myself on my vision. For decades, my eyesight was nearly perfect. I could see in crystal clear detail both up close and at a good distance. Then I started to notice words in books were getting fuzzy and distorted. I lived in denial as long as I could. Eventually, I faced reality and made an appointment with an optometrist. Reading glasses were prescribed, and immediately, I could see with clarity again.

Your eyesight is incredibly important for navigating everyday life, but there's a different kind of vision that's incredibly important for courage. This other type of vision is your vision of God. How you see God matters. What you think about Him matters. If you have a big, clear, and full vision of God, it will help you live, serve, and navigate challenges with more peace and more courage. Conversely, a small, fuzzy, and distorted vision of God is a recipe for anxiety and fear.

Let's play out this concept of your vision of God. If your vision of God includes a God who sees and cares about you, then you will have confidence that whatever your circumstances, you will never be overlooked, forgotten, or abandoned. If your vision of God includes a God who is all-powerful and active in the world, then you will have confidence that God is able to change things and trust He's working out His purposes. A big, clear, and full vision of God allows us to trust God every day and respond with courage in overwhelming crucible moments.

In contrast, a small, fuzzy, and distorted vision stirs anxiety. If you don't see God as a God who is interested or caring or as a God who speaks or as a God who is strong, then you will navigate challenges on your own and in your own very limited strength. You won't trust a small God with the big things in your life.

So how do you grow your vision of God? Here are four practices:

Steady Diet—A steady, rich diet of God's Word focused on His character and attributes is critical to growing your vision of God. You need to let any small, fuzzy, or distorted visions of God collide with the unchanging truth of God's Word. In and through God's Word, you will be grounded and reminded of the majesty and magnitude of God.

Worship Music—Biblically rooted worship music helps us remember and declare God's character. Music and worship help us more deeply process and remember who God is.

Gather—Christian community isn't optional. Church isn't optional. Intentionally engaging God's Word through preaching, teaching, and study will deepen and broaden your vision of God. Seeing and hearing others worship God, knowing how God is at work in people's lives, and hearing people choose to trust God even in difficult circumstances will deepen and broaden your vision of God. Being known and served by brothers and sisters in Christ will deepen and expand your vision of God. Serving in the community will also deepen and broaden your vision of God.

Pray—Prayer should include a declaration of who God is. You can pray (even memorize) specific Scriptures that declare the character and attributes of God. If you more deeply internalize a bigger vision of God, you will live more courageously in light of who He is.

BOTTOM LINE

Your vision of God will greatly impact how you navigate life and your level of courage. Cultivating a bigger, clearer, and fuller vision of God will give you more courage.

ACTION AND REFLECTION

Reflect on each of the four practices and take note of how you could take action to grow your courage:

Steady Diet—Do you have a steady diet of God's Word? A *plan* (what you are studying in God's Word), a *place* (where you engage God's Word), and a *time* (when you engage God's Word) are three key ingredients required to establish a regular rhythm and steady diet of God's Word.

Worship Music—Where and when do you listen to and/or engage in worship music? When you need more courage, how could worship help or be your go-to?

Gather—Are you regularly gathering in a Christian community? Gathering at church? Do others really know you? Are you serving?

Pray—Should you more actively incorporate prayer and even memorize Scripture that stirs a bigger, clearer, and fuller vision of God? (Idea: Read Psalm 103, identify at least six aspects of God's character, and declare each one in prayer.)

PRAYER

(Inspired by Isaiah 40:25–31)

Holy God, Stir in me a bigger, clearer, and fuller vision of who You are!

To whom can I compare You? Who is Your equal? I lift my eyes and look to the heavens that You created. You brought out every star one by one and called each of them by name. Because of Your great power and mighty strength, not one of them is missing.

I can't say that my way is hidden from You. I can't complain that You disregard my cause. You are the everlasting God, the Creator of the ends of the earth. You don't grow tired or weary. No one can fathom Your understanding.

You give strength to the weary. You increase the power of the weak. I hope in You, Lord, and You renew my strength. With my hope in You, I will soar on wings like eagles. I will run and not grow weary. I will walk and not faint.

I pray these things in the name of the One who is bigger, better, and more powerful than I can imagine.

19.

YOU ARE SURROUNDED

As the mountains surround Jerusalem, so the
LORD surrounds his people both now and forevermore. (Psalm 125:2)

HAVE YOU EVER felt like you can't go on? Maybe you've been
worn down by the grind? Maybe you feel all alone? Maybe
obstacles have felt too daunting and the opposition too overwhelming?

A few years ago, I spoke with a pastor who had seen God
do great things through his ministry. Nearly twenty years into
the church plant he started, he was still serving at the church.
Over the years, what was initially a fragile church plant grew
into a large, thriving church. In fact, so many new people were
coming to faith in Christ that this pastor wrote and published a
book to help new disciples get grounded in the basics of faith.

While this story of longevity and faithful perseverance
inspired me, I was more captivated by the story behind the
story. I learned that in the early days of church planting, things
got very hard for this pastor. Eventually, due to the ongoing
grind, loneliness, challenges, and opposition, he found himself
at the end of his rope. He felt very overwhelmed, and he very
much wanted to give up, quit, and pack it all in. But he didn't.

Surprised by his vulnerability, I asked him what kept him going through those early difficult days. He quickly responded that he couldn't give up because so much had been poured into him by mentors, teachers, and other courage givers in his life. The memory, reality, and legacy of their investment in his life gave him the courage and fresh energy to go on in the midst of hard days.

This story reminds me of Hebrews 12:1, one of my favorite Bible verses. It starts with the reminder, "Since we are surrounded by such a great cloud of witnesses ... let us run with perseverance the race marked out for us."

To run the race with perseverance, you need to start by remembering that you are surrounded. Specifically, you are surrounded by a great cloud of witnesses, which includes the "who's who of faith list" in Hebrews 11 — Noah, Abraham, Sarah, Isaac, Jacob, Joseph, Moses, Rahab, and the list goes on. Their examples of faith should inspire and give courage when your race gets challenging. In a sense, they are surrounding you and cheering you on as you run your race.

You are not only surrounded by this "who's who of faith list" but also by everyday courage givers who have poured into and cheered you on throughout your life.

In the difficult and dark moments of his race, the church-planting pastor was reminded of the faces and names of people who had poured into him. People who had been cheering him on and were still cheering him on.

Do some names and faces come to your mind as you think about courage givers in your life?

Being surrounded by the great cloud of witness from Hebrews 11 and hearing the cheers from everyday courage givers in your life, you can't overlook the overwhelmingly good news that Jesus Himself is cheering you on. He's your greatest cheerleader and courage giver. He loves you so much that

He died for you. Jesus walks (and runs) with you today. He modeled the way of perseverance for you. He is more for you than anyone else.

BOTTOM LINE

You are not alone. You are surrounded by saints, past and present, who are cheering you on. Jesus, the King of kings and Lord of lords, sees you and understands what you are going through, and He is personally cheering for you today. Don't give in. Never give up.

ACTION AND REFLECTION

Added to the great cloud of witnesses from Hebrews 11 are more witnesses who are cheering you on. Think back over your life. Whose example in faith has inspired you? Who has poured into you? Who has prayed for you? Who has been and is cheering you on? Make a list of at least eight to ten people.

Whether you've written down the names of grandparents, parents, family members, spouses, pastors, friends, teachers, coaches, mentors, colleagues, or congregants, there are a lot of witnesses whose examples, voices, and prayers have been (and still are) cheering you on. Consider sending a note of thanks and encouragement to people on your list (and if anyone on your list has passed from this life, send your note to their surviving spouse or children).

PRAYER

(Inspired by Psalm 125:2 and Hebrews 12:1–3)

> God who surrounds me, thank You that I am
> not alone. You are with me and all around me.
> Thank You for the men, women, and children

of faith who have modeled the way of faithful perseverance before me. Thank You for all those who have poured into me.

Remind me of their examples and voices cheering me on today.

As I run this race by Your grace and in Your strength, I choose to fix my eyes on Jesus, the pioneer and perfecter of faith. Thank You for His example in light of the joy set before Him when He endured the cross, scorning its shame, and sat down at the right hand of the throne of God. When the going gets tough for me, remind me to consider Him who endured such opposition from sinners so that I will not grow weary and lose heart.

I pray these things in the name of the author and perfecter of my faith who surrounds me.

20.

HOW'S YOUR AWE?

> I consider everything a loss because of the surpassing worth of knowing Christ Jesus my Lord, for whose sake I have lost all things. I consider them garbage that I may gain Christ. (Philippians 3:8)

IT'S HUMBLING TO read Paul's letter to the Philippians. For starters, he's in jail. He's separated from friends. His itinerant church planting ministry seems to be at a dead end. The future of his calling and ministry are uncertain, and even his own life is in serious peril.

Yet Paul is upbeat. Beyond upbeat, his joy is overflowing and contagious. In fact, he references joy at least sixteen times in this short letter. Beyond joy, Paul is also content, despite his difficult circumstances and uncertain future. He writes, "I know what it is to be in need, and I know what it is to have plenty. I have learned the secret of being content in any and every situation, whether well fed or hungry, whether living in plenty or in want" (Philippians 4:12). In other words, Paul is saying, "Whatever happens, whatever my circumstances, I'm okay."

If anyone should be discouraged, it should be Paul. Yet, Paul doesn't go down that dark hole. Instead, he's a courage giver to the Philippians. He consistently points to God's work in and through them with the goal of encouraging them. He writes, "My brothers and sisters, whom I love and long for, my joy and crown, stand firm in the Lord" (Philippians 4:1). Despite his circumstances, Paul is being a courage giver.

Even the threat of death doesn't faze Paul. He writes, "To me, to live is Christ and to die is gain" (Philippians 1:21). In other words, if I live, then I will be with Christ, and if I die, I'm even more present with Christ. For Paul, there's no problem either way. Instead of being deflated by circumstances, Paul is fueled by courage.

So what's going on with Paul? In the midst of captivity, loneliness, challenge, uncertainty, opposition, and even the possibility of death, why does Paul respond with joy, contentment, and encouragement to others?

The short answer is that Paul is jazzed about Jesus. In other words, he's been captured and captivated by the wonder of knowing, following, and walking with Jesus. He's in utter awe of Jesus. As Paul writes, "I consider everything a loss because of the surpassing worth of knowing Christ Jesus my Lord, for whose sake I have lost all things. I consider them garbage that I may gain Christ" (Philippians 3:8).

For Paul, his very difficult circumstances and very real challenges are secondary to the real prize—knowing Christ. For Paul, his mission, success, and circumstances aren't the goal of his life—it's knowing Christ.

Too often, my sense of joy, contentment, and courage have been directly related to my circumstances. If my circumstances are good, then I'm good. If my circumstances aren't good, then I'm not good. Simply hearing a mosquito in my tent at night can undo me.

I've also tried to find joy, contentment, and courage in something, in someone, or somewhere. Too often, I've forgotten the key to contentment, and courage is none of the above.

The key is Christ and the gift we have every day to know Him more.

BOTTOM LINE

Paul's joy, contentment, and courage flowed from His awe of Jesus. Nothing was more important or more central to Paul's life and ministry. Stop seeking something, someone, or somewhere to be and do what only Jesus can be and do.

ACTION AND REFLECTION

One way I've been seeking to stir my awe of Christ is to focus on His character and attributes. Specifically, I've been trying to memorize an aspect of Jesus's character and attributes for every letter of the alphabet. With this growing list committed to memory, I declare the wonder of Jesus letter by letter.

To take on this action step, begin to make your own list as you read Scripture. Spoiler alert—there are a few letters that are really hard or maybe impossible. If you need some hints, see my Jesus alphabet list in Appendix I.

Read Colossians 1:15–20. Read it a second time, but substitute the name Jesus for every reference to "his" or "him." (See the following prayer.)

PRAYER

(Inspired by Colossians 1:15–20)

> Lord, stir in me a fresh wonder and awe of Jesus. I pray Colossians 1:15–20 and declare: **Jesus** is the image of the invisible God, the firstborn of all creation. In **Jesus**, all things were created: things in heaven and on earth, visible and invisible, whether thrones, powers, rulers, or authorities. All things have been

created through **Jesus** and for **Jesus**. **Jesus** is before all things, and in **Jesus**, all things hold together. Jesus is the head of the body, the church; **Jesus** is the beginning and the firstborn among the dead, so that in everything, **Jesus** might have supremacy. For God was pleased to have all his fullness dwell in **Jesus**, and through **Jesus** to reconcile to himself all things, whether things on earth or things in heaven, by making peace through **Jesus's** blood, shed on the cross.

Forgive me for being a prisoner of my circumstances. I recognize that my sense of joy, contentment, and courage are found in Christ rather than somewhere else, in someone or something.

I pray these things in the One whose name is above all names.

21.

SEE PEOPLE

"Jesus kept looking around to see who had done it." (Mark 5:32)

"THANKS FOR ACKNOWLEDGING me."

I heard these words from a homeless man on the street who had asked me for some spare change. I had just looked him in the eye and apologetically shared that I didn't have any change to give him.

Though I didn't meet his request, the man's response indicated that my simple acknowledgment—my simply seeing him—mattered. It made me wonder how many times a day this man experienced people outright ignoring him or at least trying to avoid eye contact or conversation with him.

This connection reminded me that simply seeing people matters in a world where there's an epidemic of loneliness. Seeing people is a prerequisite for being a courage giver. If we don't see people, we won't be courage givers. And simply seeing people can give them courage.

We can all miss seeing people—even the people right in front of us. The speed of life, our propensity to focus on ourselves, our eyes constantly glued to our smartphones, and our fear of engaging with others are just some of a long list of reasons why we might not see people.

Thankfully, Jesus saw people. Though He was often surrounded and pressed by needy crowds, He saw individuals and people who were often overlooked. In the midst of a sea of people, Jesus locked eyes with a tax collector named Zacchaeus, who was perched up in a tree. On an everyday ordinary trip to get a drink of water, Jesus saw a woman at a well. And He saw beyond her posture and words, beyond cultural barriers and the prejudice of his own tribe. He saw her as a valuable person made in the image of God who had unique needs and challenges.

Every single person matters. You won't ever see someone who doesn't matter. They matter because they matter to God. They matter because they are made in God's image. They matter because Jesus died for them. They matter because they are designed to contribute to this world and maybe even to your own life.

Every single person also has a story. And somewhere in every person's story, there is a need for courage.

Seeing people starts with remembering that other people matter, that everyone has a story, and that everyone needs more courage. Being able to see people requires slowing down. It requires being present to people when we are around them. It means choosing empathy over judgment. It means not dismissing people. It means acknowledging someone with your eyes, your ears, your words, or your smile. It means keeping an eye out for people who might be overlooked. It means remembering that everyone needs more courage in some area of their life. It means being sensitive to God's prompts during your day and responding to them.

Who might God be calling you to see today? Seeing someone might just give them a boost of courage to navigate their day or even face down their giant.

BOTTOM LINE

Actually, seeing people is the starting point for being a courage giver. Despite being constantly in crowds, Jesus saw individuals. We need to slow down, be attentive to seeing people around us, and be intentional in giving courage.

ACTION AND REFLECTION

Make a point of seeing and acknowledging people during your day today. Move more slowly and put your phone down so you actually see people. Be present to the people around you. Keep count of how many people you take an extra moment to look in the eye, listen to, speak to, or encourage in some way.

PRAYER

(Inspired by Matthew 9:36)

> Lord, I affirm that everyone I see today matters because they matter to You. You looked at the crowds, which filled You with compassion because they were like sheep without a shepherd.
>
> Please slow my cadence down so I can see people in my everyday moments today. Give me Your eyes to see people and Your heart of compassion to love and encourage. Help me to be sensitive to Your prompts when I see people. Guide me in acknowledging people with my eyes, ears, words, and actions.
>
> By Your grace, may my comings and goings today help someone feel less alone, more connected, and have greater courage.

Help me to leave deposits of courage wherever I go and whatever I do.

I pray this in the name of the One who
sees me and says I matter.

WEEK FOUR

22.

CAN YOU FILL IN THE BLANK?

Moses said to God, "Who am I that I should go to Pharaoh and bring the Israelites out of Egypt?" (Exodus 3:11)

CAN YOU FILL in this blank? "I'm not _____ enough."

For most people, this isn't a time-consuming or difficult question. The answers seem to flow with surprising speed and multiple possibilities. Here are just a few examples:

- I'm not <u>old/young</u> enough.
- I'm not <u>wise or educated</u> enough.
- I'm not <u>experienced or skilled</u> enough.
- I'm not <u>extroverted or bold</u> enough.
- I'm not <u>good or pure</u> enough.
- I'm not <u>strong or courageous</u> enough.

Unfortunately, this list could go on and on. The fill-in-the-blank words may be different from person to person, but the impact is the same. These words can easily become negative self-talk in our minds. Left unaddressed, the negative self-talk often becomes toxic—your courage drains. You can feel inadequate or even disqualified. There's a very real temptation to self-select out and just stay safe on the sidelines.

This was Moses's reality. In Exodus 3, Moses encounters a burning bush. Through this burning bush that doesn't actually burn up but does audibly talk, God gets Moses's captive attention. Through the bush, God shares that He's heard and seen the misery of His people under the oppression of the Egyptians. He also shares that He has a plan to bring freedom and blessing to His people. At this point, everything must sound like great news to Moses. But then God's plan becomes personal.

In Exodus 3:10, God says to Moses, "Now, go. I am sending you to Pharaoh to bring my people the Israelites out of Egypt." When Moses hears that God wants him to lead the exodus, he doesn't think he *should* or that he even *can* do it. He responds, "Who am I that I should go to Pharaoh and bring the Israelites out of Egypt?"

Behind Moses's question, you can sense him filling in the "I'm not _____ enough" blank. After all, Moses's résumé has some serious issues and glaring shortfalls. It can be easily argued that he isn't qualified for this important and dangerous job. Born an Israelite but raised an Egyptian, Moses doesn't fully belong to either group. Then there's the fact that he is a wanted murderer and fugitive. We also know Moses has very limited resources. In fact, the sheep he's taking care of aren't even his; they are his father-in-law's. Later on, it becomes clear that he's not a great speaker with the natural skills to persuade Pharaoh to do something he doesn't want to do.

So Moses looks at himself and determines that he doesn't have what it takes to face down the most powerful man in the land. With his less-than-stellar résumé and all the negative self-talk that goes with it, Moses wants to self-select out and stay safe on the sidelines. He has no courage to move forward in obedience to God's call.

If your courage has ever drained out because of your real or perceived shortcomings, then pay attention to how God responds to Moses. In Exodus 3:12, God looks past Moses's self-appraisal and says these game-changing words, "I will be with you." In other words, God is saying, "You may not be enough, but I am enough. Me being with you is enough. I am—my character and my presence—your qualification."

Moses isn't buying it. He's still desperate to find a way out. He says to God, "Suppose I go to the Israelites and say to them, 'The God of your fathers has sent me to you,' and they ask me, 'What is his name?' Then what shall I tell them?" In other words, "What's my qualification?"

At this point, God again makes Moses's qualifications very clear. He says to Moses, "I AM WHO I AM. This is what you are to say to the Israelites: 'I AM has sent me to you.'" God wants Moses to get his eyes off of himself, off his shortcomings (real and perceived), and even off his calling. God is seeking to bring Moses's eyes onto the Caller. To do what God is asking him to do, Moses must get his eyes off himself and place his confidence in God.

So let's go back to your fill-in-the-blank. Has God called you to do something? It may very well have your knees knocking and self-doubts stirring. If so, where are your eyes looking? If your courage comes from looking at yourself, you are in trouble. That's called pride. The opposite is also true. If your lack of courage comes from looking at yourself, you are in trouble of a different kind. You aren't looking at who is with you—God.

How might your outlook and courage change if you look to God—His character and His presence with you?

BOTTOM LINE

It's easy to fill in the "I'm not _____ enough" blank. Filling in the blank drains courage. As Jesus's followers, we need to get our eyes off ourselves and focus on God. Who He is, and His presence with us, are our ultimate qualifications and source of courage.

ACTION AND REFLECTION

As you reflect on what God has called or is calling you to do, what are your "I am not _____ enough" blanks? Make a list. How do these words impact your courage?

Respond to each blank by declaring that God is enough. Declare the words of 2 Corinthians 12:9 with a prayer like this: God, as I look at my shortfalls—real and perceived, I declare, "'Your grace is sufficient for me, for your power is made perfect in my weakness.' Therefore, I will boast all the more gladly about my weaknesses so that Christ's power may rest on me."

PRAYER

(Inspired by 2 Corinthians 3:5 and 12:9)

> Lord, forgive me for putting my eyes squarely on myself. I cannot qualify myself before You in anything for anything. My competency and courage ultimately come from You—Your character, Christ's work on the cross, the Holy Spirit's ongoing work and gifts in me, and Your ongoing presence with me. Even and especially in my weaknesses, Your grace is sufficient. Your power is made perfect.
>
> Through faith in You and by Your grace, I obediently choose to look to You and to follow You.
>
> I pray these things in the powerful name of the great I AM.

23.

REMEMBER FAITH MARKERS

Because of the LORD's great love we are not consumed, for his compassions never fail. They are new every morning; great is your faithfulness. (Lamentations 3:22–23)

BACK IN THE OLD Testament days, when God did something significant, people would often mark the event by giving the place a special name or building an altar.

For example, when the Jordan River was at flood stage, God miraculously parted the river to allow all of Israel to safely cross into the Promised Land. After all the people had miraculously crossed, God told Joshua to take twelve stones from the middle of the Jordan and create a memorial altar. God knew there were more trials ahead, and He knew when things got difficult that, the memorial would help His people remember His power, faithfulness, character, and plan for all generations.

Celebrating and remembering God's work was common practice in Old Testament days. The names and memorials became an educational and encouragement tool for future generations. When a young person asked about the pile of rocks on a memorial altar, they would then hear and be encouraged by another story of God's provision and protection. These stories were fuel for courage.

Unfortunately, we have lost touch with this meaningful tradition. When God does something amazing, we don't name a place or create a memorial. In fact, we might be going so fast or could be so distracted we don't even take notice of the amazing thing God did. This comes at a cost to courage. If we don't remember what God has done in the past or if we don't even take notice of what He's doing in the present, then we won't be encouraged in the moments when we need courage.

Without a doubt, we need to avoid making idols out of what God has done or where He's done it. We need to focus and save worship for God Himself. However, we will benefit by being more intentional in reflecting, remembering, and celebrating what God has done and is doing in our lives. One of the most repeated failures of the Israelites was their forgetfulness of who God was and what He had done.

When you are at a low point or in a crucible moment that requires courage, you can find more courage by remembering what God has already done. Remembering doesn't put God in a box where He must do the same thing again in different circumstances. But remembering does remind you of God's limitless power, absolute faithfulness, unchanging character, and prevailing plan for your life.

One of Mary Oliver's short poems, "Sometimes," provides a profound template for remembering God's faithfulness and work in our lives. She writes, "Pay attention. Be astonished. Tell about it."[4] Too often, we move too fast to pay attention to what God has done or is doing. As a result, we aren't astonished, and we have nothing to tell about.

Be sure to take time to remember and share stories and examples of God's faithfulness with others.

---

4. Mary Oliver, *Red Bird* (Boston: Beacon Press, 2008).

BOTTOM LINE

We need to pay more attention to God's past and present work in our lives. If we do, our perspective will change. Our attitude will reset. We will find more courage, and we will become courage givers to others.

ACTION AND REFLECTION

Here are four action steps to remember and leverage faith markers:

1. Take some time to pay attention and reflect on God's faithful work in your life. Make a list of at least four or five faith markers where God has been faithful or done special work in your life. If you journal, look back over your journal entries for reminders. Hint: Consider a regular practice of journaling in a notebook or even recording notes on your phone to capture God's faithfulness.

2. Spend some time giving God praise and thanksgiving for His faithfulness and these specific examples.

3. Consider if there's a creative way you might tangibly remind yourself of these faith markers to fuel praise, thanksgiving, and courage. Here's one idea: Find a rock to represent each faith marker, use a marker to write a word on each rock to represent God's work, and place the rocks where they will encourage you.

4. How might you share some of these faith markers to encourage others (i.e., family, grandchildren, church friends, mentees, work colleagues, people you long to see follow Jesus)?

PRAYER

(Inspired by Lamentations 3:22–23 and Revelation 19:11)

Faithful God, throughout history and my life, You have demonstrated Your limitless power, absolute faithfulness, unchanging character, and prevailing plan.

Forgive me for my inattention and forgetfulness.

Prompt me to pay attention. Stir in me awe and wonder to be astonished.

Remind me to keep telling myself and to creatively tell others about You and Your ongoing work in my life. May who You are, what You have done, and what You are doing fuel my courage to follow Jesus today and every day.

I pray these things in the name of the one who is called Faithful and True.

24.

LEAN IN

Though one may be overpowered,
two can defend themselves.
A cord of three strands is not quickly broken.
(Ecclesiastes 4:12)

HAVE YOU EVER felt like the weight of the world was on your shoulders? It's an overwhelming and isolating feeling. This kind of weight squeezes out courage.

In the garden of Gethsemane, Jesus was feeling the weight of the world on His shoulders. This was His crucible moment. It's impossible for us to comprehend or understand what this struggle must have felt like for Jesus, but we need to take note.

Jesus didn't give in or give up. He chose obedience even when it meant separation from the Father. He followed the Father's way even when it meant submitting to religious and earthly authorities bent on His capture and public torture. Despite carrying the weight of atonement for the sins of the world, Jesus followed the path set out for Him.

I've often wondered why Jesus, in this crucible moment, brought His inner circle of Peter, James, and John with Him. The most obvious answer from the text is that He wanted them to pray. However, when we read the account, we learn Jesus's inner circle kept falling asleep—even while Jesus was literally sweating blood in response to the weight and pressure He was experiencing. As we know, letting Jesus down wasn't an isolated incident for the disciples. It was part of an ongoing pattern in their time with Jesus. They just didn't fully get it or get Him.

So why would Jesus still bring His inner circle to the garden even when He likely knew they'd let Him down? Why not just save the disappointment and go it alone?

I believe Jesus chose to invite His inner circle because He consistently leaned into the community. Day after day, Jesus chose to live, love, lead, serve, and suffer in the context of community. He chose to do so even when His community was far from perfect.

Jesus's example should encourage all of us to lean into community. The Christian life should never be a solo endeavor. Going solo is dangerous, even at the best of times. If we feel that life is extra hard, extra lonely, or extra tiring right now, Jesus's example tells us to lean into community rather than out of it. Jesus's example tells us to lean into community even when the community isn't perfect. And by the way, no community is perfect.

You can choose to lean out of the community or lean into the community. Leaning out of community leads to isolation and insecurity. In difficult moments, keeping your thoughts, worries, and feelings isolated internally doesn't breed courage, life, or anything positive. By contrast, leaning into the community brings deeper connection, strength, and, ultimately, courage.

So who or where do you need to lean into today? Here are four ideas.

1. **Lean into Jesus.** Of all the people who have walked this earth, Jesus understands you and your situation most. Jesus cares about you and your situation. Jesus can

help you and your situation. He's the best friend you've got.

2. **Lean into your family, friends, team, or board.** Who are the "safe but not soft" people you can reach out to and share your needs or situation? Safe people can be trusted, are quick to listen, and slow to judge. But you don't want someone who is soft. You want someone who is compassionate but will ultimately encourage and point you in the way of truth and obedience. Take a step of faith and share how you are doing and your current challenges, and then pray together. Who can you invite into your garden of Gethsemane moment? Who should you be leaning into on a regular basis?

3. **Lean into professionals.** A spiritual mentor can help you listen to God. A counselor can help you process and cope. A doctor can monitor physical and mental health. A coach can help you find solutions and determine the next steps. A consultant can help move projects forward. Is there someone you need to lean into right now?

4. **Lean into peers.** For an ongoing community, find an hour or two per month with two or three peers (in-person or online if needed). Ask these six questions: How are you really doing? What can you celebrate right now? What are you learning? What are you grieving? What's hard? How can we pray? Then

pray. This simple format breeds community and courage.

BOTTOM LINE

In difficult moments, to keep connected every day, follow Jesus's example by leaning into the community—even when the community isn't perfect. Community breaks isolation and stirs courage.

ACTION AND REFLECTION

Who do you need to lean into today? (Review the four ideas presented in this chapter.)

What next step will you take to lean into community?

PRAYER

(Inspired by Matthew 1:23, Ecclesiastes 4:12, Proverbs 27:17, and John 15:5)

Lord, thank You that I am not alone. You are with me right now and always.

I admit that I can't navigate this moment of my life on my own. So, following Jesus's example and by Your grace, I recognize that a cord of three strands is not quickly broken. I am choosing to lean into You and into community—even if the community isn't perfect.

Show me safe people to lean into who will give me courage and sharpen me as iron sharpens iron. In this season, please guide me, protect me, bless me, and encourage me through the community.

I pray these things in the name of the One who calls me friend.

25.

SPIRITUAL BILLIONAIRE

> Praise be to the God and Father of our Lord Jesus Christ, who has blessed us in the heavenly realms with every spiritual blessing in Christ. (Ephesians 1:3)

CAN YOU IMAGINE what it might be like to be a billionaire? I'm sure there are many pressures. There are also likely endless temptations that come with so much wealth. But I'm also pretty sure you'd never be anxious when the restaurant server drops the bill off at your table at the end of dinner. After all, whatever the bill, you could afford to pay not just for dinner but to buy the restaurant, demolish it, and then rebuild it over and over again.

Few people in the world can relate to having a billion dollars, but every follower of Jesus is what Tim Keller calls a spiritual billionaire.[5] You are a spiritual billionaire because of the magnitude of what Christ has done for you and in light of your identity as a joint heir with Christ.

Ephesians 1:3–14 provides a glimpse into the riches you've been given in Christ. Here's a sampling:

---

5. Timothy Keller, *Encounters with Jesus: Unexpected Answers to Life's Biggest Questions* (New York: Penguin Books, 2015), 144–45.

- You are **blessed** in the heavenly realms with every spiritual blessing in Christ.

- You are **chosen** in Him before the creation of the world.

- You are **holy** and **blameless** in God's sight.

- You are **predestined for adoption** through Jesus Christ.

- You are **redeemed** by Jesus's blood for the forgiveness of sins.

- You have the **riches of God's grace** lavished on you.

- You are **included in Christ** upon hearing the message of truth.

- You are **marked in Him with a seal**, the promised Holy Spirit.

This list is incredible, but it's just a start to painting a picture of your enormous wealth in Christ. There is much more that Christ has done. There is much more that you have already received. There is much more that you will receive because of Christ.

So how might knowing you are a spiritual billionaire help you find more courage?

Just like having a billion dollars should relieve you of worry about paying for your dinner bill, knowing you are a spiritual billionaire should dramatically reduce your fear of what people think, say, or post about you. Knowing you are a spiritual billionaire should give you the courage to speak up or step forward. Knowing you are a spiritual billionaire should dramatically reduce your fear of risk and give you the energy to press forward. Knowing you are a spiritual billionaire should dramatically increase your generosity in all things. No external force, problem, or challenge can diminish the riches you have in Christ.

What God has done in Christ—both for and in you—is the richest and deepest well of courage you will be able to find!

BOTTOM LINE

Knowing you are a spiritual billionaire should ground you in a confidence that overflows into courage. After all, what can actually diminish you or shake you if you are a spiritual billionaire?

ACTION AND REFLECTION

Read Ephesians 1:3–14. Circle, underline, or write out every identity statement listed. Reflect on each statement. How could you more deeply internalize each statement?

PRAYER

(Inspired by Ephesians 1:3–14 and 1 Peter 1:4)

> Lord, the truest thing about me is what You say about me.
>
> You have blessed me. You have chosen me for a purpose. You have adopted me—I am Yours! You have redeemed and forgiven me through Christ. You have predestined me for Your purposes. You have included me as Your child. You have guaranteed my inheritance—a living hope that can never perish, spoil, or fade.
>
> By Your grace, help me to live today and face whatever may come as a humble,

grateful, generous, and courageous spiritual billionaire.

I pray these things in the name of the One who has given me a living hope.

26.
POSTURE MATTERS

> "Blessed are the poor in spirit, for theirs is the
> kingdom of heaven." (Matthew 5:3)

KING DAVID'S RÉSUMÉ was pretty impressive. A gifted musician and poet. He killed a lion, a bear, and Goliath. A successful warrior. A skilled strategist. A called, chosen, and anointed leader. A man after God's own heart. The list could go on and get much longer.

You might expect that David's résumé would produce some swagger, pride, and independence. However, he prays a very similar prayer twice in the Psalms that points to a very different kind of posture.

Here's the prayer: "As for me, I am poor and needy; come quickly to me, O God. You are my help and my deliverer; Lord, do not delay" (Psalm 70:5; see also Psalm 40:17).

In this prayer, David demonstrates an unexpected posture in three ways:

> 1. Humility—David's posture is one of humility. He firmly proclaims that he is not a self-made or self-sufficient man. Instead, he acknowledges he's both poor and needy. He seems to be someone who desperately needs God's help.

2. Dependence—David clearly acknowledges that, ultimately, God is his help and his deliverer. He chooses to depend on God rather than his limited strength.

3. Trust—David chooses to trust in God, His character, and His coming provision.

For a stark contrast, let's take a brief look at Saul's posture. Rather than a posture of humility, Saul exudes entitlement. He believes he should be king no matter what. Rather than dependence, Saul tries to independently maintain his reign by attempting to kill David and by being disobedient to God's instructions. Rather than trust, fear is the driving force in Saul's life. This is demonstrated in his paranoia toward David as well as his frantic and, at times, bizarre attempts to take matters into his own hands repeatedly.

Sometimes, it's tempting to think that courage is about believing in yourself or finding a reserve of strength somewhere deep inside yourself. David's posture shows another way. David's way starts with humbly admitting his poverty and limitations and then dependently declaring and trusting in God's unlimited capacity.

It may be counterintuitive, but there's actually freedom in admitting up front that you don't have what is needed. On my own, I know I don't have what it takes to stand before a holy God or do battle with the evil one. On my own in this crazy and complex world, I know I don't have what it takes to solve the problems I face at work. On my own, I'm in deep trouble. But with and in Christ, everything changes. Fresh courage comes by humbly depending on and trusting God.

BOTTOM LINE

You will face challenges that are much bigger than your capacity. The best thing you can do isn't to believe in yourself or try to find more courage from the inside. The best thing you can do is to choose a posture of humility and look outside to depend on and trust in God and His unlimited strength.

ACTION AND REFLECTION

Start each day with a prayerful posture of humility, dependence, and trust. Pray your own prayer or pray Psalm 70:5—"As for me, I am poor and needy; come quickly to me, O God. You are my help and my deliverer; Lord, do not delay."

Your prayer could involve a physical posture of praying on your knees or with your hands open to demonstrate your humility and dependence.

PRAYER

(Inspired by Psalm 70:5, John 15:5, Philippians 4:8, and Ephesians 5:18)

I start most days with what I call a "Prayer of Dependence" (I also call it a "Prayer of Incompetence") that reflects the posture of Psalm 70:5. Here's a general outline of my daily prayer:

> Dear God, I need You.
>
> Before my day even starts, I admit I'm in over my head today. For all that needs to be done today, my limited strength isn't enough. For the complexities in my own life and our world, I'm short on wisdom. For the trials and temptations that will come, I cannot withstand them on my own.

STEVE A. BROWN

You are the vine, and I am a branch; apart from You, I can do nothing. I can make it through anything with You.

I ask that You would fill me with Your Spirit and live Your life in me today. By Your grace and power, produce fruit in me that would glorify You, bless others, and bless me.

I pray this prayer in the name of the One who is my strength, my help, and my deliverer.

27

ARMOR UP

Be strong in the Lord and in his mighty power.
Put on the full armor of God, so that you can
take your stand against the devil's schemes.
(Ephesians 6:10–11)

I JUST DIDN'T see it coming. It had been a great day. My heart
was full after seeing several breakthroughs that were clear
answers to prayer. Then, wham! My day suddenly and unex-
pectedly shifted. I went from a mountaintop moment to a very
unexpected, complex, and difficult valley that lasted weeks.

During this dark valley season, there were times when I
wondered if I was literally going to make it. I was having trouble sleeping and teetered on the edge of exhaustion. My body
didn't feel good. Fears stirred, and I was discouraged to the
point of wanting to give up.

Thankfully, I was able to persevere and, over time, emerge
from this deep valley into a new season. Yet as I reflected on
what had happened, I could clearly see evidence that this had
been a spiritual attack from the evil one. It was an incredibly
clever and perfectly timed scheme designed for maximum
damage.

When I talk about a "spiritual attack," there are two ditches
that need to be avoided. The first ditch is to be consumed by
and even paranoid about the work of the evil one. It's tempting

to see the evil one behind every corner and challenge. The truth is he's not behind everything that goes wrong. The other ditch is to be in denial or ignorant that the evil one is actively working to distract, discourage, divide, and destroy. He is an active and gifted schemer. Both ditches need to be avoided. We need to live in the tension that the evil one is at work but recognize that not everything is the work of the evil one.

Here are three takeaways from my experience:

1. The evil one is prowling around like a roaring lion looking for someone to devour (1 Peter 5:8), so be spiritually alert and spiritually aware. Don't be surprised he's at work—even in response to positive and forward steps. As the adage goes in hockey, "keep your head up" to avoid getting blindsided. In other words, be spiritually alert!

2. We are in a spiritual battle, and God has given us armor to wear—so wear it (Ephesians 6:11–17). Wearing armor gives courage, protection, and strength in battle. As Ephesians 6:13 says, "Put on the full armor of God, so that when the day of evil comes, you may be able to stand your ground, and after you have done everything, to stand."

3. Be intentional in prayer, and invite others to pray proactively for protection and as intercessors in difficult moments. As Ephesians 6:12 says, "Our struggle is not against flesh and blood, but against the rulers, against the authorities, against the powers of this dark world and the spiritual forces of evil

in the heavenly realms." Your smarts and strength are not enough for this kind of battle. Prayer is critical.

Remember that Jesus is bigger and stronger. The ultimate victory has already been won. As Colossians 2:15 says, "Having disarmed the powers and authorities, he made a public spectacle of them, triumphing over them on the cross."

BOTTOM LINE

The evil one is real and at work. Don't be paranoid or ignorant. Be spiritually alert. Armor up. Pray. Know Jesus reigns over all.

ACTION AND REFLECTION

Start each day by praying on the armor of God in Ephesians 6:13–17. Use the following prayer as a model.

PRAYER

(Inspired by Ephesians 6:12–17)

Lord, I recognize there is a spiritual battle, and the evil one is active in ways that I cannot always see. I don't want to underestimate or overestimate his schemes.

Thank You for the armor You provide to protect me and help me stand firm whatever comes. By faith, I put on the helmet of salvation and the breastplate of righteousness. I buckle up the belt of truth, and I take up the shield of faith to extinguish the flaming arrows of the evil one. I take up the sword of the Spirit, which is Your Word, and I ask that You bring Your Word to my mind. Take my feet and use them to share Your peace wherever I go and whatever I do today.

I pray this in the name of the One who is my protector and has already won victory over darkness.

28.

PRAY

> Let us then approach God's throne of grace with confidence, so that we may receive mercy and find grace to help us in our time of need. (Hebrews 4:16)

DO YOU THINK you might have more courage if you knew that someone was *continually* mentioning you in their prayers? What would happen to your courage if you knew someone was *constantly* praying for you?

The Thessalonians, who had experienced suffering and were enduring persecutions and trials, had someone who was both *continually* and *constantly* praying for them. At the beginning of his first letter, Paul reminded them that we "continually mention you in our prayers" (1 Thessalonians 1:2). In his second letter, Paul writes, "We constantly pray for you" (2 Thessalonians 1:11).

Paul's *continual* and *constant* prayers had a very real spiritual impact, but they also reminded the Thessalonians that in their difficulties, they were neither forgotten nor alone. Paul remembered them and was standing (or perhaps kneeling) with them in prayer. Paul's prayers were also a reminder that their challenges were not beyond the awareness or power of God. Learning that Paul was faithfully praying for them would have been a great source of encouragement.

The discipline and practice of praying on behalf of others is often called intercessory prayer. This kind of prayer is something all Jesus's followers can do. It's not reserved for a special group or gifting. In a world where every Jesus follower will face trouble and many will experience extreme challenges, it is both a necessity and privilege to faithfully pray for others.

Though we do not always see an immediate or even direct response to our prayers, we are called to pray. Prayer is partnering with God in His work. Knowing that people are praying gives courage. Knowing that others are praying breaks isolation and is a reminder to every Jesus follower that they are part of and connected to the global body of Christ. Knowing that others are praying is a reminder that we can entrust our very real challenges to a faithful, good, and able God.

So if you desire to be a courage giver, then pray. Be faithful in bringing others and their needs before the throne of God. And follow Paul's example by letting people know that you are praying for them. Send a short and simple text or note that says you are praying. These brief touchpoints in communication often arrive at just the right moment.

BOTTOM LINE

Prayer is a key practice for courage givers. God listens to and responds to prayer. Knowing someone is praying breaks isolation, builds connection, and stirs courage. Be faithful and intentional in praying for others—and let them know.

ACTION AND REFLECTION

Make a list of people you know who might need courage. Think of people who are ill, suffering, lonely, facing opposition, contemplating taking new steps of faith or making major decisions, navigating new situations, or experiencing a life transition.

As you look at your list, make a plan to pray regularly. What is a doable frequency that you can commit to praying for each person? The main thing is to pray. Remember to pray that they would have courage and choose to follow Jesus even when their knees might be knocking. Let them know regularly that you are praying for them.

PRAYER

(Inspired by Hebrews 4:16)

> Lord, Thank You for allowing us to approach Your throne with boldness and confidence for our needs and the needs of others.
>
> Please teach me how to pray for others. Please stir in me a longing to faithfully pray for others.
>
> Please receive my prayers as a declaration of dependence on You. May my prayers express my trust in You and bring courage to others, knowing You are the all-powerful helper, wise guide, gracious redeemer, miraculous provider, powerful protector, and faithful source of true courage.
>
> I pray these things in the name of the One who is our advocate, actively sharing our needs with the Father.

JESUS THROUGH THE ALPHABET

GROWING A BIGGER, fuller, and clearer vision of Jesus gives courage. Grounded in Scripture, the list below shares an attribute of Jesus for most letters of the alphabet. Read through the list. Is there an attribute that you need to remember, thank God for, or share with someone?

JESUS …

Advocate (1 John 2:1)

Bread of Life (John 6:35)

Cornerstone (Ephesians 2:20)

Deliverer (Romans 11:26)

Emmanuel, God with us (Matthew 1:23)

Friend (John 15:13–15)

Good Shepherd (John 10:11)

Holy One (Mark 1:24)

I am (John 8:58)

Judge (2 Timothy 4:1)

King of kings (Revelation 17:14)

Lord of lords (Revelation 17:14)

Mediator (1 Timothy 2:5)

Name above every name (Philippians 2:9)

Omega (Revelation 22:13)

Peace (Ephesians 2:14)

Redeemer (Ephesians 1:7)

Savior (Luke 2:11, 1 John 4:14–15)

Truth (John 14:6)

Unchanging (Hebrews 13:8)

Vine (John 15:1)

The Way (John 14:6)

Word (John 1:1)

.

APPENDIX II:
ENCOURAGING WORDS

THERE ARE OVER 150 positive attributes and characteristics listed below that can help you encourage others. As you think of a specific person, what words below best describe them? Use these words in your verbal or written encouragement.

Accommodating
Administrative
Adventurous
Agile
Apostle
Approachable
Architect
Artistic
Assertive
Attitude

Bold
Bridgebuilder
Brilliant

Caring
Communicator
Compassionate
Competent
Confident

Connector
Courageous
Creative
Cultural Intelligence

Decisive
Dedicated
Dependable
Detailed
Determined
Diligent
Discerning
Disciplined

Efficient
Encourager
Energetic
Enterprising
Entertaining
Entrepreneur

Evangelist
Excellence
Exceptional
Expertise

Faithful/Faith-filled
Flexible
Focused
Forthright
Friendly
Fun

Generous
Gentle
Goodwill
Graceful/Gracious
Grounded
Growing

Healer

STEVE A. BROWN

Helper
Holy
Honest
Hopeful
Hospitality
Humble
Humorous

Innovative
Insightful
Inspiring
Intelligent
Intentional
Imaginative

Joyful
Justice

Kind
Knowledgeable

Leader
Learner
Listener
Loving
Loyal

Magnetic
Mature
Mercy
Modest
Motivating/Motivated
Multi-tasker

Natural
Networker

Nonanxious presence
Nurturing

Observant
Optimistic
Organized
Outgoing

Passion
Patient
Peace
Persistent
Persuasive
Playful
Polite
Positive
Prayerful
Prepared
Principled
Proactive
Problem Solver
Productive
Prophet
Protective
Purposeful

Qualified
Quality

Realist
Reflective
Refreshing
Researcher
Resourceful
Respectful

Responsible

Selfless
Self-awareness
Sensitive
Servant/Serving
Shepherd
Skilled
Strategic
Strong
Synergy

Tactful
Talented
Teacher
Teamwork
Tested
Thankful
Trusted

Uncompromising
Understanding
Unique
Upbeat

Versatile
Vibrant
Victorious
Virtuous

Warm
Wholehearted
Wholesome
Willing
Wise
Writer/Written

ACKNOWLEDGMENTS

Courage givers are true gifts from God. Over the years, I have been blessed with many men, women, and children who, by God's grace, have seen me through ups and downs by loving me, walking alongside me, faithfully praying, frequently reminding me of God's faithfulness, and pointing me toward Jesus. At key moments when I needed it most, they called me out and told me about God and His limitless power, absolute faithfulness, unchanging character, and prevailing plan for my life. Thank you for surrounding me and cheering me on in this race that's been marked out for us!

As I write these final words of this book, I need to single out two courage givers in particular who served alongside me as faithful board members, mentors, and friends. The first is Keith Anderson. Keith, thank you for faithfully coming alongside me and being a safe and wise friend who carefully listens, faithfully prays, and lovingly encourages me as a leader. And Miller Alloway, thank you for faithfully cheering me on in life and leadership for over twenty years! Thank you specifically for patiently and persistently cheering me on to keep writing. To you both—your impact on my life and in the lives of so many others near and far is truly more than you can imagine.

ABOUT STEVE A. BROWN

Dr. Steve Brown lives out his passion to invest in the next generation of Jesus-centered leaders as President of Columbia Bible College in Abbotsford, British Columbia, Canada.

Over the last twenty-five years, Steve has invested thousands of hours coaching, teaching, and walking alongside leaders from Canada, the USA, and around the world. He served as President of Arrow Leadership for over a decade, and he's the author of *Jesus-Centered—Focusing on Jesus in a Distracted World*, *Leading Me—Eight Keys to a Leader's Most Important Assignment*, and *Great Questions for Leading Well*.

Steve's been married to Lea for over twenty-five years and is the proud dad to three young adults. Running, biking, hiking, and traveling are his longtime passions. You can reach him at presidentsoffice@columbiabc.edu.

ABOUT COLUMBIA BIBLE COLLEGE

Our heartbeat is to help shape the next generation of wholehearted followers of Jesus.

We are committed to helping students lean into their faith and launch their lives in ways that glorify God.

With three tracks to choose from, Church Ministry and Biblical Studies, Discipleship, and Marketplace/Careers, we aim for every student to cultivate spiritual vibrancy grounded in God's Word, grow in Christlike character, experience deeply rooted community, and develop passion and skills for serving for a lifetime.

Whatever you choose—a one-year certificate, two-year diploma, or four-year degree—you are building a foundation for whatever you do and wherever you go.

Learn more: www.columbiabc.edu.

www.ingramcontent.com/pod-product-compliance
Lightning Source LLC
Chambersburg PA
CBHW050823090426
42738CB00020B/3459